# WORLD
# HISTORY

Authors: Anita Ganeri, Hazel Mary Martell and Brian Williams

Illustraters: Martin Camm, Richard Hook, Rob Jakeway, John James, Shane Marsh, Roger Payne, Mark Peppé, Eric Rowe, Peter Sarson, Roger Smith, Ross Watton, Michael Welply and Michael White

Consultant Editors: Brian Williams and Brenda Williams

This edition designed by Starry Dog Books.

This is a Parragon book
This edition published in 2006

Parragon
Queen Street House
4 Queen Street
Bath BA1 1HE, UK

Copyright © Parragon Books Ltd 2003

Printed in Indonesia

British Library Cataloguing-in-Publication Data

A catalogue record for this book is available from the British Library.

ISBN 1-40546-939-0

# WORLD
# HISTORY

p

# Contents

# Discovering the Past

**W**HAT IS HISTORY? In its broadest sense, history is the story of people – the study of our past. Some historians look at important events, such as wars, revolutions and governments, while others are interested in ordinary people's lives. Henry Ford, the American car manufacturer, once said "History is bunk", but most people would disagree. Our lives today are shaped by decisions and actions made decades, centuries or even thousands of years ago. By understanding the past, we may be able to gain a more balanced view of the present.

Alabaster canopic jars from the tomb of an ancient Egyptian. We can find out a lot about ancient peoples from their religious beliefs. The Egyptians believed in life after death, and filled their tombs with things they thought they would need in the afterlife.

THE BASIC AIMS of history are to record and explain our past. Historians study a range of written and oral (spoken) evidence. Combined with archaeology (the study of things people have left behind them, such as buildings and objects), historians interpret the facts to build up a picture of the past.

The first people to study history seriously were the ancient Greeks. In the 5th century BC, the Greek historian Herodotus (known as "the Father of History") set out to write a true and systematic record of the wars between the Greeks and the Persians. He hoped to preserve the memory of past events and show how two peoples came into conflict with one another.

A cuneiform writing tablet. Cuneiform was the first system of writing. The oldest tablets date from about 5,000 years ago. Ancient written records like this are the raw materials of history. Before writing, history was passed on by word of mouth.

> Navigational instruments like this one were used in the 15th century by explorers in search of new lands. Throughout history, new inventions have changed the world and increased our knowledge.

∧ A historian studying the life of a medieval knight would look at the buildings of the time, such as this Crusader castle in Syria.

The scientific study of archaeology only began in the 18th century. Archaeologists today investigate even the tiniest fragments left behind by our ancestors to help create a more complete picture of the past.

Interpreting the evidence is the most fascinating part of a historian's or archaeologist's job. Historians, however, must always be aware of bias or prejudice in the things that they read or write. Bias means being influenced by a particular point of view, while prejudice means "judging before" – before you have all the facts. Historians themselves are influenced by the times they live in. Modern historians try to avoid applying the values and beliefs of the present to their interpretations of the past.

History is not just concerned with the distant past. It is the story of our lives – what is news today will be history tomorrow. Change can be sudden and dramatic, and long-held ideas may be overturned.

< Pictures can tell us much about life in the past, showing us people's homes, clothes, jobs and food. This painting was done for the Duc du Berry (1340–1416).

> This carved ivory mask was worn as an ornament by the oba, or king, of Benin – a powerful African empire from the 14th to 17th centuries. The wealth and sophistication of Benin was expressed in its art.

# The Ancient World

## FROM PREHISTORIC TIMES TO AD 500

THE VAST PERIOD of time from 2.5 million years ago to AD 500 saw the appearance of the first human beings and the creation of the first civilizations. Our earliest ancestors appeared in Africa some 2.5 million years ago, having evolved from man-apes who came down from the trees and learned to walk upright on two legs.

OVER THOUSANDS OF YEARS, people learned how to make fire to keep themselves warm and to cook their food, how to hunt and how to make tools. The first-ever metal tools and weapons were made in the Near East about 7,000 years ago.

Throughout the world, early people lived by hunting animals and gathering wild fruit, roots and nuts to eat. By 10,000 years ago, however, an extraordinary change was taking place People learned how to grow their own crops on patches of land and to raise their own animals for food. For the first

| c. 2.5–2 million years BC | c. 40,000 BC | c. 10,000 BC | c. 8000 BC | c. 3500 BC The | c. 2580 BC | c. 2500 BC | c. 1850 BC |
|---|---|---|---|---|---|---|---|
| *Homo habilis* appear in Africa. They are the first people to make tools. | Our direct ancestors, *Homo sapiens sapiens*, appear in many parts of the world. | The last Ice Age comes to an end. | Farming begins and the first towns are built in the Near East. | Sumerians of Mesopotamia invent writing and the wheel. | The Great Pyramid at Giza, Egypt, is built. | The Indus civilization in ancient India is at its height. | Abraham leads his people from Ur to Canaan. |

time in history, people began to build permanent homes, followed by towns and cities.

By about 5000 BC, the world's first civilizations began to emerge along the banks of rivers where the land was extremely rich for farming. The Sumerians, Assyrians and Babylonians built magnificent cities and temples on the fertile plains between the Tigris and Euphrates rivers. The ancient Egyptians flourished along the river Nile. By about 500 BC, important civilizations had also appeared in India, China, Persia and in North and South America.

The great age of ancient Greece and Rome is known as the Classical period. These two mighty civilizations played a major role in shaping the modern world. From Greece came discoveries in politics, philosophy and science. These were spread further afield by the Greek conqueror Alexander the Great, and by the Romans, who were great admirers of Greek culture and knowledge.

The Romans added achievements of their own and, by the 1st century AD, ruled over the most powerful empire ever seen. But by AD 500 their empire had fallen. The Middle Ages had begun.

| 1600–1100 BC | 753 BC | c. 605–562 BC | 269–232 BC | 221 BC | 27 BC–AD 14 | AD 286 | AD 476 |
|---|---|---|---|---|---|---|---|
| Mycenaeans dominate mainland Greece. | Traditional date for the founding of Rome. | Reign of King Nebuchadnezzar II, who rebuilds the city of Babylon. | Reign of Emperor Ashoka Maurya in India. | Shi Huangdi unites China; he is its first emperor. | Augustus rules as the first Roman emperor. | The Roman empire is divided into west and east. | The last western emperor of Rome is deposed. |

# The First Humans

THERE HAS BEEN life on Earth for some 300 million years, but the first humanlike creatures appeared about 7 million years ago. These "man-apes" came down from the trees in which they, like other primates, lived. They walked on two legs and used tools.

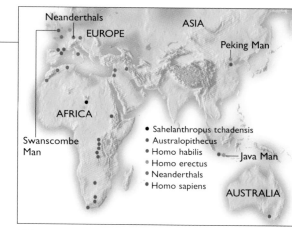

This map shows the location of important fossil remains of early hominids and humans. *Homo erectus* as the first great colonizer, spreading out of Africa. Scientists still argue whether *Homo sapiens* first appeared in Africa or developed in other parts of the world.

• Sahelanthropus tchadensis
• Australopithecus
• Homo habilis
• Homo erectus
• Neanderthals
• Homo sapiens

THE TOUMAI SKULL found in Chad, in Africa, in 2002 may be a clue to the oldest hominid or humanlike creature known. Some scientists think it is 7 million years old. The fossil record then jumps to about 4 million years ago, when the Australopithecines lived in Africa. The most complete skeleton of an

A set of Australopithecine footprints was found by Mary Leakey in 1978, preserved in volcanic ash at Laetoli, Kenya. It showed that early hominids walked upright on two legs.

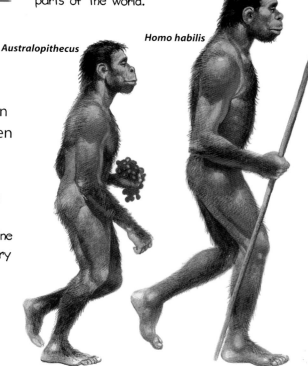

*Australopithecus*

*Homo habilis*

**c. 4 million years ago**
*Australopithecus* (meaning "southern ape") appear in Africa. They walk upright on two legs instead of on all fours.

**c. 2.5–1.5 million years ago**
*Homo habilis* ("handy man") appear in Africa. They are the first people to make and use tools.

**c. 1.5 million years ago**
*Homo erectus* ("upright man") appear in Africa. They are the first people to spread out of Africa.

**c. 120,000 years ago**
The Neanderthals, a sub-species of *Homo sapiens* ("wise man"), appear in Africa, Asia and Europe. They are the first humans to bury their dead.

*Australopithecus* was found in Ethiopia in 1974. The individual, nicknamed "Lucy", died about 3 million years ago, aged about 40. She was as tall as a 10-year-old.

FIRE
People first made fire by striking two flints together. It gave them protection from wild animals, allowed them to cook food, and provided heat and light.

The first true human beings, known as *Homo habilis* (Latin for "handy man"), appeared about 2.5 million years ago. They had bigger brains and made tools from sticks and stones. A million years later another species, *Homo erectus* ("upright man") had appeared and gradually spread out of Africa into Europe and Asia. These early humans made better tools (for hunting), built shelters and also used fire.

Many scientists believe that modern humans, *Homo sapiens* ("wise man"), evolved from these hominids. Two species lived side by side: Neanderthal people and modern people. By about 20,000 years ago the Neanderthals had died out, and modern humans, *Homo sapiens sapiens*, were living on all of the continents.

*Homo erectus*

*Homo sapiens neanderthalensis*

*Homo sapiens sapiens*

◄ As early people evolved, they gradually became less like apes and more like humans. They developed larger brains, and bodies designed for walking upright, with longer legs than arms. Standing upright left their hands free for using tools and weapons.

**35,000 years ago**
omo sapiens sapiens "modern humans") are ving in many parts of e world, including ustralia.

**c. 30,000 years ago**
The Neanderthals die out as modern humans appear in Asia and Europe.

**c. 20,000 years ago**
Modern humans have crossed from Asia into the Americas.

# The First Farmers

FOR MOST of human history, people found food by hunting wild animals and gathering berries, nuts and roots. They lived as nomads, following the herds of animals they hunted. Then, about 10,000 years ago, a huge change took place. People learned how to grow crops and rear animals for food.

INSTEAD OF HAVING to roam farther and farther afield to find food to eat, people found they could grow enough for their families on a small patch of land. This meant that they had to settle in one place all year round and build permanent homes. These people were the first farmers. Their farming settlements grew to become the first villages, which in turn grew to become the first towns.

On farms in Europe in about 3000 BC, people made clay pots, which they fired in kilns and used for storing grain and water. They used stone axes to fell trees and clear land, and stone sickles to harvest crops. They also spun wool and wove it into cloth on looms (far left).

**c. 10,500 BC**
The first clay pots are made in Japan.

**c. 8000 BC**
Farming begins in the Near East in an area known as the Fertile Crescent, and in Southeast Asia. Sheep are domesticated in Iraq.

**c. 7000 BC**
Farming develops in Central and South America. Clay pots for storing grain and water are made in the Near East and Africa.

**c. 6500 BC**
The oldest-known textiles are woven at Çatal Hüyük in Turkey.

## DESERT ROCK ART

Cave paintings in Algeria dating from 10,000 years ago show people hunting giraffe, hippos and elephant. Later paintings show farmers tending herds of cattle. After about 3000 BC, when the Sahara's climate became drier, the rock art shows desert animals, such as camels.

The first farms developed in the Near East and Europe in a region known as the Fertile Crescent (shaded area). Farming spread throughout Europe and western Asia, but it developed independently in the rest of Asia and in the Americas.

Plants and animals that are grown or raised by people are known as "domesticated". The first domesticated plants and animals were developed from those found in the wild. Wheat and barley, which had grown wild in parts of the Near East for thousands of years, were two of the first crops to be domesticated. People collected seeds from these wild plants and sowed them in ground dug over with deer antlers. (Ploughs were not invented until about 6,000 years ago.) The next year, the crop was harvested and the grain ground into flour to make bread, which was baked on hot stones. Farmers also learned how to tame wild sheep, goats and pigs and breed them, so they no longer had to go hunting for their meat.

**c. 6000 BC**
Beer, made from grain, is brewed in the Near East.

**c. 5000 BC**
Farming is adopted in China and Egypt and spreads to Europe. It also begins in India, along the Indus and Ganges river valleys.

**c. 4400 BC**
Horses are domesticated in Eastern Europe and used for riding for the first time.

**c. 4000 BC**
The first ploughs, made of sharp, forked sticks, are used in the Near East. The earliest plough marks discovered were in Mesopotamia.

# Mesopotamia and Sumer

ONE OF THE world's earliest civilizations grew up on the fertile plains between the rivers Tigris and Euphrates, in what is now Iraq. The area became known as Mesopotamia, "the land between the two rivers". About 5000 BC, the Sumerians settled in southern Mesopotamia.

◀ Writing was invented in Sumer in about 3500 BC, as a way of keeping temple records and merchants' accounts. This clay tablet shows the cuneiform ("wedge shaped") symbols used to represent words.

▼ A great ziggurat, or stepped temple, was built in the city of Ur by King Ur-Nammu in about 2100 BC.

Shrine to the Moon god Nanna at the very top

◀ The Sumerians made splendid jewellery from gold and silver inlaid with semi-precious stones. Craft workers also made furniture, wine cups and musical instruments. Such treasures were found in the Royal Tombs at Ur when they were excavated.

As earlier mud-brick temples fell into ruin, new temples were built on top, raising the platform higher and higher

| c. 5000 BC | c. 4000 BC | c. 3500 BC | c. 2900–2400 BC |
|---|---|---|---|
| Early Sumerians begin to farm in Ubaid, southern Mesopotamia (Iraq). | The start of the Uruk Period. The Sumerians learn how to smelt metal. They use sailing boats on the Tigris and Euphrates rivers. | The Sumerians invent writing and the wheel. They discover how to make bronze from copper and tin. | The Early Dynastic Period. Kings are established in the main Sumerian cities. |

THE FERTILE LAND of Mesopotamia was ideal for growing crops. Farmers soon learned how to build irrigation canals to bring water from the rivers to their fields. As more food was grown, the population increased, and by about 3500 BC some villages had grown into thriving towns. The towns of Ur and Uruk grew to become cities, and then independent city-states.

The cities were ruled by Councils of Elders, who appointed *lugals* (generals) to lead the armies in times of war. As wars between rival cities became more frequent, the lugals' powers grew, and from about 2900 BC the lugals were kings, ruling for life.

In the centre of each city stood a temple to the city's patron god or goddess. The Sumerians believed the gods controlled every aspect

The Sumerians may have built reed houses similar to those of the Marsh Arabs, who live on the banks of the river Tigris in southern Iraq.

of nature and everyday life. It was vital to keep the gods happy with daily offerings, or they might send wars, floods or disease to punish the people.

The Sumerians were expert mathematicians. They had two systems of counting. One was decimal, like the system we use today; the other used units of 60 (the Sumerians were the first to divide an hour into 60 minutes). They also devised a calendar, a complex legal system, and used the wheel for pot-making and on carts. But their most important invention was writing.

## GILGAMESH

The most famous of the Sumerians' many myths and legends is the epic of King Gilgamesh and his quest to find the secret of eternal life. He learns that a plant that gives immortality grows at the bottom of the sea, but the plant is stolen by a snake before he can use it.

| 2400–2100 BC | c. 2300 BC | c. 2100 BC | c. 2000 BC |
|---|---|---|---|
| ...umer is conquered ...y the Akkadians, ...en by the ...utians. | The Sumerian city of Agade dominates the region. | The city of Ur reaches the height of its power under King Ur-Nammu. | The epic of Gilgamesh is first written down. The city of Ur is destroyed by the Elamites. Sumerian civilization comes to an end. |

# Ancient Egypt

**W**ITHOUT the life-giving waters of the river Nile, ancient Egypt would have been a barren desert, too dry for farming. The river gave the ancient Egyptians drinking water, as well as water for irrigation. It also deposited rich soil along its banks each year when it flooded.

ALONG THE Nile's banks, farmers grew wheat and barley (for bread and beer), flax (for linen), and fruit and vegetables. They also raised cattle, sheep and goats. So vital was the river that the Greek historian Herodotus described ancient Egypt as the "gift of the Nile".

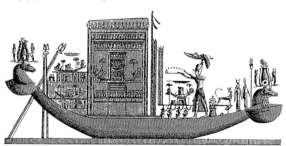

Boats were the main form of transport, used for fishing, hunting, and carrying cargo and passengers. When a pharaoh died, his body was taken by barge to his tomb.

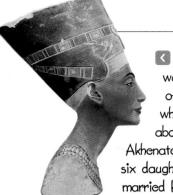

Queen Nefertiti was the chief wife of King Akhenaten, who ruled Egypt in about 1364–1347 BC. Akhenaten and Nefertiti had six daughters, one of whom married King Tutankhamun.

The first villages of ancient Egypt appeared some 7,000 years ago. In time, these small settlements increased and two kingdoms were created – Lower Egypt in the Nile delta and Upper Egypt along the river valley. In about 3100 BC, King Menes, the ruler of Upper Egypt, united the two kingdoms and built his capital at Memphis. He established the first dynasty (line of kings) of ancient Egypt.

Farmers at work in Egypt. The farmers' year was split into three parts: the Inundation (July to November) when the Nile flooded, the Growing Season (December to March) and Harvest (March to July). When the flood made farmwork impossible, farmers were sent to work on the royal buildings.

| c. 5000–3100 BC | c. 4000 BC | c. 3200 BC | c. 3100 BC | c. 3100–2686 BC |
|---|---|---|---|---|
| Predynastic Period in Egypt. Several cultures appear along the Nile valley. | Boats on the Nile use sails for the first time. | Early hieroglyphs are used in Egypt. | King Menes unites Lower and Upper Egypt. | Archaic Period (Dynasties 1 and 2). |

## PYRAMID CONSTRUCTION

No one knows exactly how the pyramids were built. It is thought that stone blocks, some as heavy as cars, were pulled to the site on wooden sledges dragged by teams of workers, then hauled up a series of spiral mud and brick ramps into place. Layer by layer the pyramid grew. Finally, the capstone at the top was added and the whole structure covered in white limestone casing blocks. Then the ramps were dismantled.

The king was the most powerful person in ancient Egypt. He was worshipped as the god Horus. From about 1554 BC, the king was given the title "pharaoh", from the Egyptian words 'per aa', meaning "great house". Two officials, called viziers, helped him govern and collect taxes. Officials also ran the major state departments – the Treasury, the Royal Works (which supervised the building of pyramids and tombs), the Granaries, Cattle and Foreign Affairs. Every aspect of Egyptian life was under the pharaoh's control.

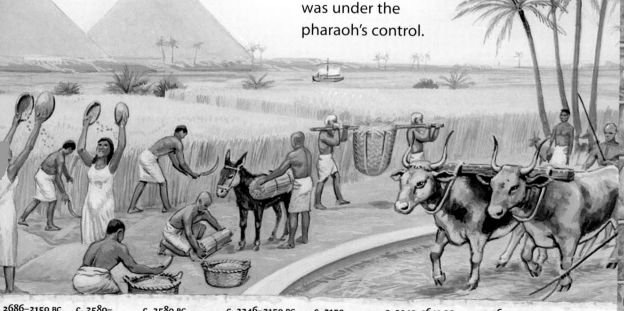

| 2686–2150 BC | c. 2589– 2566 BC | c. 2580 BC | c. 2246–2150 BC | c. 2150– 2040 BC | c. 2040–1640 BC | c. 1640–1552 BC |
|---|---|---|---|---|---|---|
| Old Kingdom (Dynasties 3 to 6). The first of the pyramids are built. | Reign of King Khufu (Dynasty 4). | The Sphinx and Great Pyramid at Giza (a tomb for King Khufu) are built. | Reign of King Pepi II (Dynasty 6), the longest reign in history. | First Intermediate Period (Dynasties 7 to 10). | Middle Kingdom (Dynasties 11 to 13). King Mentuhotep II reunites Egypt and restores order. | Second Intermediate Period (Dynasties 14 to 17). The Hyksos people from Asia overrun Egypt. |

# Life and Death in Egypt

THE ancient Egyptians believed in life after death. They buried their dead in tombs filled with items for use in the afterlife. These tombs, with their paintings and treasures, tell us much about these remarkable people.

The walls of tombs were covered with paintings of gods and goddesses. Shown here are Osiris, the god of the dead, on the left and Atum, the Sun god, on the right.

THE EGYPTIANS BELIEVED that for a person's soul to prosper in the next world, the body had to be preserved. This is why they made mummies. Dead bodies were embalmed and dried, then wrapped in linen strips and placed in coffins. The finest tombs were those of the kings. Some were buried in pyramids, but later rulers of Egypt were laid to rest in rock tombs, in the Valley of the Kings. Most tombs were ransacked

Hieroglyphics was the system of picture-writing used in ancient Egypt. Each picture, or hieroglyph, stood for an idea or a sound. Hieroglyphs were written on walls as well as on sheets of papyrus. People trained to write them were called scribes.

The Great Temple at Abu Simbel was built by King Ramesses II. Four gigantic seated statues of the king guard the entrance.

When a body was mummified, the dead person's liver, lungs, stomach and intestines were removed, wrapped and stored in containers called canopic jars. The head-shaped lids represented protective gods.

| c. 1552–1085 BC | c. 1479–1425 BC | c. 1364–1347 BC |
|---|---|---|
| The New Kingdom in Egypt (Dynasties 18 to 20). | Reign of King Tuthmosis III. The Egyptian empire is at the height of its power. | Reign of King Akhenaten. |

by robbers, but one survived largely intact. It was discovered and opened in 1922 by British archaeologist Howard Carter. The tomb belonged to the boy-king Tutankhamun, and inside were priceless treasures of a vanished world.

Egypt's greatness lasted for over 2,500 years. The Egyptians were skilled in maths and astronomy, and drew up a calendar of 365 days. They had a system of picture-writing called hieroglyphics. Their doctors were the best in the world. They built pyramids and temples bigger than any structures seen before, and traded overseas in large ships. It is not surprising that even peoples who later conquered Egypt, such as the Romans, stood in awe of the Egyptians' achievements.

▷ Tutankhamun's gold death mask covered the face of the dead king. His body lay wrapped in linen inside a nest of three coffins, encased in a stone sarcophagus and protected by four wooden shrines.

| 1347–1337 BC | c. 1289–1224 BC | c. 1085–664 BC | c. 664–332 BC | 332 BC | 323–30 BC |
|---|---|---|---|---|---|
| Reign of King Tutankhamun. | Reign of King Ramesses II. | Third Intermediate Period (Dynasties 21 to 25). | The Late Period (Dynasties 26 to 30). c. 525–404 BC The Persians rule as Dynasty 27. | Alexander the Great takes control of Egypt. Founds Alexandria (331 BC). | Rule by the Ptolemies until Cleopatra kills herself in 30 BC. Egypt then becomes a province of the Roman empire. |

# Ancient China

THE earliest civilizations in China grew up along the banks of three major rivers – the Chang Jiang, Xi Jiang and Huang He. Farmers used the water to irrigate their crops, but often suffered bad floods.

FROM ABOUT 2205 BC, China was ruled by a series of dynasties (ruling families). The first for which experts have good evidence is the Shang dynasty, which began in about 1766 BC. The Shang ruled for more than 400 years, until they were conquered by the Zhou.

Zhou rule lasted until 221 BC. During this time many wars were fought between the rival

◁ Early copper "coins" were shaped like tools, and were different in each state. Under Shi Huangdi, all coins were made round with a hole in, so they could be strung together.

kingdoms that made up the Zhou lands. But it was also a period of economic growth, with Chinese silk, precious jade and fine porcelain being traded abroad.

By 221 BC, the kingdoms of China had been at war for more than 250 years. Gradually, the Qin (or Ch'in), a war-like dynasty from the northwest, united the country and established the empire that gives China its name. The first emperor of the united China, Shi Huangdi, reorganized government and standardized money, weights and measures. A road and canal network was built to link up various parts of

◁ A terracotta soldier from the enormous underground tomb of Shi Huangdi, who was buried in 210 BC with all that he needed to survive the afterlife. This included a vast army, 10,000 strong, of life-sized clay soldiers.

▷ The Great Wall of China (built 214–204 BC) was more than 2,250 km long, 9 m high and wide enough for chariots to pass along. Thousands of peasants worked on the wall. If their work was below standard, they were put to death.

**Convicted criminals were used as a workforce**

| c. 1766–1027 BC | 1027–256 BC | c. 551 BC |
|---|---|---|
| The Shang dynasty rules China. | The Zhou dynasty rules China. | Birth of the great teacher, Confucius. |

## CONFUCIUS

The philosopher Confucius was born in about 551 BC, at a time when wars were frequent. He dedicated his life to teaching people how to live in peace. His teachings formed the basis of the Chinese civil service up to the beginning of the 20th century.

| Tree | Moon | Bird | Sun | Horse | |
|------|------|------|-----|-------|--|
| 木 | 月 | 鳥 | ○ | 馬 | About 1500 BC |
| 木 | 月 | 鳥 | ○ | 馬 | Before 213 BC |
| 木 | 月 | 鳥 | 日 | 馬 | After AD 200 |

The earliest Chinese writing was found on oracle bones (Shang dynasty). Gradually the picture symbols became more abstract in form.

the country, and the Great Wall of China was built across the northern border to keep out the hostile Hsung Nu (the Huns). Shi Huangdi was a brilliant but ruthless general and politician, putting scholars to death if their ideas did not match his own. The Qin dynasty was overthrown in 206 BC, four years after Shi Huangdi's death.

Watch towers provided shelter for the army from attackers

Chinese nobles came to watch the construction

Earth was packed down into mud blocks, then lined with cobbles

A pulley on a bamboo scaffold lifted earth from surrounding works

Workers carried heavy materials with a balanced yoke

Conscripted soldiers worked as overseers

**481–221 BC**
The so-called Warring States Period, when most of China is in a state of civil war.

**221 BC**
Shi Huangdi unites China and founds the Qin dynasty. He becomes China's first emperor.

**212 BC**
The Burning of the Books by Shi Huangdi – his suppression of ideas that did not match his own.

**210 BC**
Death of Shi Huangdi.

**206 BC**
The Qin dynasty collapses and the Han dynasty rules China until AD 9.

# The Babylonians

**B**ABYLON, once a small kingdom of Mesopotamia, first grew powerful under the rule of King Hammurabi (c. 1792–1750 BC). He extended Babylon's frontiers to include Sumer and Akkad, and rebuilt the city of Babylon, making it the capital of the new empire.

> Legend says that the Hanging Gardens of Babylon were built for Nebuchadnezzar's Persian wife, Amytis, because she missed the green hills of her homeland. The gardens were one of the Seven Wonders of the ancient world.

< King Nebuchadnezzar II (ruled c. 605–562 BC) captured Syria and Palestine, and forced many of the people of Jerusalem to live in captivity in Babylon.

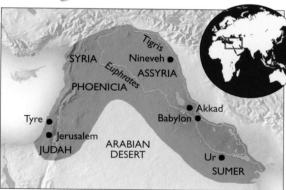

SYRIA
Tigris
Nineveh ●
ASSYRIA
Euphrates
PHOENICIA
Tyre ●
Akkad ●
Babylon ●
Jerusalem ●
JUDAH
ARABIAN DESERT
Ur ●
SUMER

This map shows the extent of the Babylonian empire under Nebuchadnezzar II. His army defeated the Egyptians to take Syria.

HAMMURABI was a just and diplomatic ruler. He is famous for his code of law, the oldest surviving in the world. The laws were recorded on stone pillars for all to see. After his death, Babylon was invaded by the Hittites, Kassites, Chaldeans and Assyrians. The Assyrian king Sennacherib destroyed the city in 689 BC. But Babylon regained its former glory during the 6th century BC under King Nebuchadnezzar II. The king conquered a huge empire and made the city perhaps the grandest in the ancient world.

The awe-inspiring city of Babylon stood on the banks of the river Euphrates (near Baghdad in modern-day Iraq). The capital of the Babylonian empire, it was a major trading centre and a flourishing religious complex, especially for the worship of the god Marduk, the city's patron god. In fact,

| c. 1894 BC | c. 1792–1750 BC | c. 1595 BC | c. 1595–1155 BC | c. 1126–1105 BC | c. 731–626 BC | c. 626–529 BC |
|---|---|---|---|---|---|---|
| The Amorite people establish the minor kingdom of Babylon in Mesopotamia. | Reign of King Hammurabi. Babylon first rises to power. | Babylon is plundered by the Hittites, then falls to the Kassites. | The Kassites rule Babylon. | Nebuch-adnezzar I reigns. | The Assyrians and Chaldeans fight for control of Babylon. | Babylon re-emerges as a major power in the Near East. |

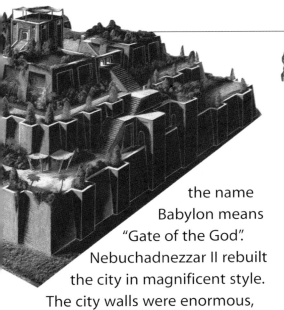

## BABYLONIAN SCIENCE
The Babylonians were excellent mathematicians and astronomers. They drew the oldest known map of the world, and were the first to use a system of weights (c. 2600 BC). The metal weights were shaped like lions.

☑ The blue-tiled Ishtar Gate was the northern entrance to Babylon. It was named after the goddess of love and war. Bulls and dragons, symbols of the god Marduk, decorated the gate.

the name Babylon means "Gate of the God". Nebuchadnezzar II rebuilt the city in magnificent style. The city walls were enormous, and there were eight massive bronze gates. The grandest, the Ishtar Gate, opened on to the Processional Way, which linked the great Temple of Marduk inside the walls to an important religious site outside the city. At the New Year's festival, statues of the gods were paraded along this route. Nebuchadnezzar also built a grand palace that became known as "the Marvel of Mankind".

| c. 626–605 BC | c. 605–562 BC | c. 597 BC | 586 BC | c. 539 BC |
|---|---|---|---|---|
| King Nabopolassar defeats the Assyrians and rules Babylon. Babylonian army, under Nebuchadnezzar defeats Egypt to win Syria. | Nabopolassar's son Nebuchadnezzar II rules Babylon. | Nebuchadnezzar conquers Judah (southern Palestine) and puts down three rebellions there. | Nebuchadnezzar destroys Jerusalem and exiles its people to Babylon. | Babylon is conquered by the Persians and becomes part of the mighty Persian empire. |

# Ancient Greece

BY ABOUT 800 BC, Greece saw the rise of a new civilization that transformed the ancient world. Its influence has lasted to the present day. Ancient Greece was divided into small, independent city-states, each with its own government and laws. The two most important were mighty Athens and Sparta.

◄ Pericles was leader of Athens from 443–429 BC. The most famous and popular politician of the "Golden Age", he ordered the rebuilding of Athens after its destruction by the Persians.

MOST CITY-STATES were ruled by a group of wealthy nobles (an oligarchy). Resentment led to revolts, and absolute rulers (tyrants) were appointed to restore law and order. Then, in about 508 BC, a new type of government was introduced in Athens. It was called democracy, meaning "rule by the people", and gave every male free man a say in how the city should be run. Many countries today are democracies, but with votes for all.

The Classical Period (when Greek culture was at its most splendid) lasted from about 500 BC to 336 BC. During that time, Greece was involved in two long-running wars. In 490 BC the Persians invaded. The Greek city-states joined

▶ The Greek army depended on its hoplites, or foot soldiers. Hoplites carried heavy round shields and long spears for stabbing the enemy. The split, skirt-like tunics allowed easy movement.

◄ In battle, Greek hoplites formed a phalanx – a block of soldiers eight or more rows deep.

The phalanx advanced in formation, spearpoints bristling, scattering the enemy foot soldiers

forces and eventually defeated them in 449 BC. One of the most famous battles took place at Marathon in 490 BC. A messenger named Pheidippides ran the 40 km back to Athens carrying news of the Greek victory. His run is immortalized in the modern marathon race.

But peace did not last. In 431 BC war broke out between Athens and Sparta (the Peloponnesian Wars). After laying siege to Athens, the Spartans starved the Athenians into submission. In 404 BC Athens was forced to surrender.

◀ The Parthenon was built on top of the Acropolis (a high hill in Athens) in the 5th century BC. It was dedicated to Athena, goddess of wisdom.

Life in Sparta was very different from life in Athens. Spartan men were trained to be fearless warriors, ready to defend the city-state from invaders and to keep the population under control. Every male Spartan had to train for war. Boys as young as seven were sent away to army camp, where strict discipline and harsh conditions turned them into the toughest fighters in Greece. Girls, too, were encouraged to be fit and strong.

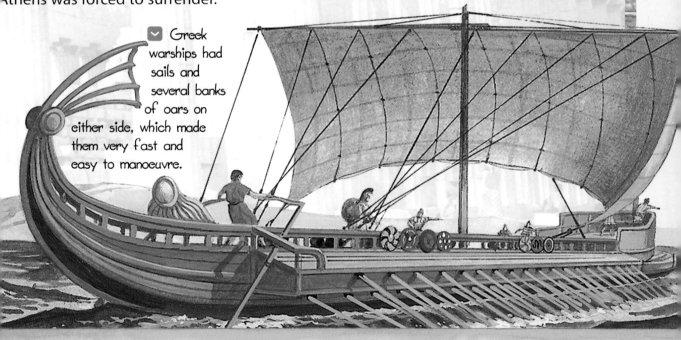

▽ Greek warships had sails and several banks of oars on either side, which made them very fast and easy to manoeuvre.

# Greek Culture

GREEK CIVILIZATION lasted far longer than the Greek city-states. Greek influence on politics, philosophy, art and architecture, language and literature had a huge effect on Roman culture and can still be felt today. Many ideas about science and art come from ancient Greece.

▶ Greek vases were beautifully decorated with detailed scenes from daily life and stories from mythology. Much of our knowledge about the ancient Greeks comes from vases and vessels.

THE ANCIENT GREEKS were great scholars, thinkers and teachers. At first they answered questions about life and nature with stories about the gods. Later, they started to look for practical and scientific ways of making sense of the world about them. Their scholars were called philosophers, which means "lovers of knowledge"; they included Socrates, Plato and Aristotle.

Drama and sport played a very important part in the lives of the ancient Greeks. Greek theatre grew from the performance of songs and dances at an annual festival dedicated to Dionysus, the god of wine. These performances were acted out by a group of men called a chorus. At first, plays were performed in a town's market place. Later, open-air theatres were built all over Greece (many can still be seen).

▶ At the Olympic Games, throwing the discus was one of five events in the pentathlon (the others were running, jumping, wrestling and javelin throwing). The winner of this demanding competition was declared the best all-round athlete at the games. The ancient Olympics ended in AD 395. The modern Olympic Games were begun in 1896.

| c. 500–336 BC | 490–449 BC | 479–431 BC | 447–438 BC |
|---|---|---|---|
| The Classical Period. Greek culture reaches its height. | The Persian Wars. The Greeks are victorious. | The Golden Age of Athens, a time of great prosperity and achievement for the city. | Parthenon temple is built in Athens. |

▶ Socrates (c. 469–399 BC), the son of an Athenian sculptor, was one of the most influential of all ancient Greek philosophers. He taught people to think about good and evil. Some people did not approve of his ideas, however, and he was forced to commit suicide.

Sport was important not only as a form of entertainment, but also as a way of keeping men fit and healthy for war. There were many competitions for athletes. The oldest and most famous was the Olympic Games, held every four years at Olympia in honour of the chief god, Zeus. For the five days of the games, a truce was called between the city-states to allow the athletes safe passage to Olympia. Athletes trained hard for months before the games. Discipline was strict and breaking the rules harshly punished. But for the winners it was worthwhile. Their prize was a simple olive crown cut from a sacred tree, and a hero's welcome, fame and fortune when they arrived back home.

▶ The Greeks developed two main styles of column for their grand public buildings and temples: Doric (top) and Ionic (centre). A third, more elaborate style, called Corinthian (bottom), was introduced in Roman times.

▼ Greek actors were all men. They wore different masks and costumes for characters that were happy, sad, male, female, old or young. The Greeks were the first to build theatres; the largest could hold an audience of 18,000 people.

31–404 BC
thens and
parta fight the
eloponnesian
ars. Sparta
ns with
ersian help.

430 BC
Plague
devastates
Athens.

371 BC
Sparta is
defeated by
the Greek
city-state of
Thebes.

362 BC
The Thebans are
defeated at the
battle of
Mantinea by the
Spartans and
Athenians.

338 BC
The Greeks are defeated
by the Macedonians at
the battle of Chaeronea.
This spells the end of
Greek independence.

336–30 BC
The Hellenistic
Period.
Alexander's
conquests spread
Greek culture.

147–146 BC
Greece becomes
part of the
Roman empire.

# Alexander and the Persians

AFTER THE squabbles following the Persian Wars, Macedonia became the dominant force in Greece. Its young king, Alexander, led his armies on an epic march of conquest, crushing the Greeks' traditional enemies, the Persians.

The Persian army's greatest strength lay in its archers and cavalry troops. But it was no match for Alexander's battle tactics.

THE PERSIAN homeland was in what is now Iran. The Persians had come to rule an empire that stretched eastward to India and as far west as Turkey. Great Persian kings, such as Cyrus the Great, commanded huge and efficient armies. Darius I (521–486 BC) built fine roads for carrying messages quickly across the empire, which he reorganized into provinces called satrapies. From 499 BC, Persia turned against the Greeks, but in 480 BC its invasion fleet was defeated at the battle of Salamis.

Power then swung towards Greece. In 338 BC Macedonia's warrior king Philip II gained control of all the Greek states by victory at Chaeronea. When Philip was murdered in 336 BC, his son Alexander became king, aged 20. It took Alexander just 13 years to conquer the largest empire in the ancient world, spreading Greek (and Persian) culture far and wide.

The city of Persepolis, built by Darius I, was the magnificent capital of the Persian kings. The ruins of the city lie near Shiraz in modern-day Iran. When Alexander captured Persepolis in 331 BC, he burned the splendid royal palace to the ground.

| 549 BC | 539 BC | 526 BC | 521–486 BC | 499–479 BC | 356 BC | 334 BC | 333 BC |
|---|---|---|---|---|---|---|---|
| Cyrus the Great of Persia conquers Lydia. | Persians conquer Babylon. | Cambyses of Persia conquers Egypt. | Reign of Darius I, Persia's "king of kings". | Persians led by Darius I and Xerxes try, but fail, to conquer Greece. | Alexander is born; becomes king in 336 BC after Philip II is murdered. | Alexander's army invades the Persian empire. | Alexander defeats Darius III's huge Persian army at the battle of Issus. |

In 334 BC Alexander led his army against the Persians. He wanted not only to conquer their lands, but also to replenish his royal treasuries. In 333 BC he defeated the Persian king Darius III at the battle of Issus, and by 331 BC had conquered the whole of Persia and become its king. To strengthen the ties between the two peoples, Alexander included Persians in his government. He also wore Persian clothes and married a Persian princess, Roxane. He went on to invade India, defeating King Porus at the battle of the river Hydaspes. It was to be his final expedition. His exhausted army refused to go on, and Alexander was forced to retreat to Babylon. He died there of a fever in 323 BC, aged 32. After his death, the empire was divided among his leading generals.

Alexander on his great warhorse, Bucephalus.

The map shows the extent of Alexander's empire and the routes he took to conquer the east.

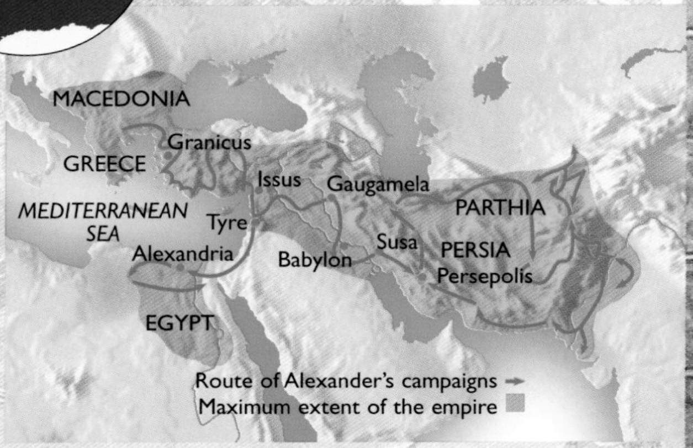

MACEDONIA
Granicus
GREECE
Issus
Gaugamela
MEDITERRANEAN SEA
Tyre
PARTHIA
Alexandria
Babylon
Susa
PERSIA
Persepolis
EGYPT

Route of Alexander's campaigns →
Maximum extent of the empire ■

| ? BC | 331 BC | 327 BC | 323 BC |
|---|---|---|---|
| xander quers pt. | Alexander defeats the Persians at the battle of Gaugamela. | Alexander reaches India. He is forced to turn back in 324 BC. | Alexander dies in Babylon. War between his generals; empire is divided. |

# The Celts

CELTIC PEOPLES spread westward across Europe from about 800 BC. They lived in tribal groups, settling in hill-forts and farms. The Celts were unable to unite against a common enemy – the formidable Roman legions.

⬆ Maiden Castle was one of the strongest Ir[?] Age hill-forts in Britain. Approaching invaders could be seen a long way off, and the fort's concentric earthworks made it difficult to capt[?]

THE CELTS were brave and fearless warriors, but they were equally skilled at metal-working, making beautifully decorated weapons, jewellery and drinking cups. They were also gifted storytellers, passing down stories of their gods and history by word of mouth. Roman writers recorded details of Celtic life and culture. They reported

⬆ Celtic craftworkers made beautiful metal objects, such as this harness decoration. Many highly decorated Celtic artefacts have survived.

that the Celts worshipped many different gods and goddesses, and offered sacrifices in their honour. Religious rituals and ceremonies were performed by priests, called druids. In charge of each of the Celtic tribes was [?] chieftain. One of the most famous was Vercingetorix, a chieftain of the Arveni, a tribe in central Gaul (France). In 52 BC, he led a successful rebellion against the Romans, but was later defeated by Julius Caesar's well-trained army.

Many Celtic tribes built huge hilltop forts surrounded by massive protective earthworks, where they lived safe from attack. Victory in battle was celebrated with feasts that could last for several days, drinking and the recital of long poems telling of the deeds of Celtic heroes and gods. Their greatest god wa[?] Daghdha, the "Good God", who

| c. 600–500 BC | c. 400 BC | 390 BC | 225 BC | 58–50 BC | 52 BC |
|---|---|---|---|---|---|
| Celtic culture develops in Austria and later in France. | The Celts build farms and hill-forts in southern and western Europe. | The Gauls (French Celts) sack the city of Rome. | The Romans defeat the Gauls at the battle of Telamon in Italy. | Julius Caesar conquers all of Gaul (France). | Vercingetorix leads a revolt against the Romans in Gaul, but is defeated by Caesar. |

controlled the weather and the harvest and brought victory in battle.

Celtic warriors were famed and feared for their bravery in battle. Wars frequently broke out between rival Celtic tribes – a weakness that helped the Romans to overwhelm them more easily.

## BOUDICCA

The Roman emperor Claudius invaded Britain in AD 43. Some Celts fought back fiercely. In AD 60, Boudicca (or Boadicea), queen of the Iceni, a Celtic tribe in eastern Britain, led a revolt against the Romans. The Celts burned London and killed some 70,000 Romans. But her army was defeated in AD 61, and Boudicca killed herself by drinking poison.

AD 61
Boudicca is defeated in a revolt she leads against the Romans in Britain.

Safe within a hill-fort, families lived with their animals in circular wooden huts. The huts were thatched and had walls of mud-plastered sticks. A huge iron cooking-pot hung over the fire in the centre.

# The Romans

ACCORDING to legend, the city of Rome was founded in 753 BC by the twin brothers Romulus and Remus. The boys were abandoned by their uncle to die on the banks of the river Tiber in central Italy. But they were rescued by a she-wolf, and later found and raised by a shepherd.

TO REPAY THE SHE-WOLF, Romulus and Remus vowed to build a city in her honour, on the Palatine Hill where she had found them. In a quarrel about the city boundaries, Remus was killed and Romulus became the first king of Rome.

From humble beginnings as a small group of villages, Rome grew to become the capital of the most powerful empire the western world had ever seen.

At first Rome was ruled by kings. Then in about 509 BC, King Tarquin the Proud was expelled from Rome, and for the nex 500 years Rome was run as a republic. Power passed to the Senate, a law-making body made up of nobles and headed by two senior officials, called consuls. They were elected each year to manage the affairs of the Senate and the army. By about 50 BC, Rome had conquered most of the lands around the

⬇ Octavian, the first emperor of Rome, was known as Augustus, or "revered one". A great politician, he reformed every aspect of government and restored peace and prosperity to Rome.

⬆ This fresco, or wall painting, comes from Pompeii, a seaside town in Italy that was destroyed in AD 79 by a volcanic eruption. Many buildings, however, were preserved under the ash and lava that smothered the town.

| 753 BC | c. 509 BC | 264–146 BC | 49 BC |
|---|---|---|---|
| The traditional date for the founding of Rome. | The founding of the Roman Republic. | The Punic Wars between Rome and Carthage in North Africa. Carthage is destroyed. Rome controls the Mediterranean. | Julius Caesar seizes power to become dictator of Rome. In 44 BC he is assassinated. |

◄ Julius Caesar, a brilliant Roman general, defeated his rivals in Rome to seize power as dictator in 49 BC. He was assassinated on March 15, 44 BC.

Mediterranean. But rivalry between army generals plunged Rome into civil war. In 27 BC, Octavian, the adopted son of Julius Caesar, became the first Roman emperor, charged with restoring peace. Under the emperors, Rome gained control of much of Europe, North Africa and the Near East.

## HANNIBAL

From 264 to 146 BC, Rome waged a series of wars, called the Punic Wars, against the Phoenician city of Carthage in North Africa, to gain control of the Mediterranean. In 218 BC, the Carthaginian general Hannibal led a surprise attack on the Romans. He marched over the Alps into Italy with 35,000 men and 37 elephants. Carthage was eventually defeated.

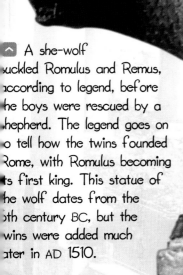

▲ A she-wolf suckled Romulus and Remus, according to legend, before the boys were rescued by a shepherd. The legend goes on to tell how the twins founded Rome, with Romulus becoming its first king. This statue of the wolf dates from the 5th century BC, but the twins were added much later in AD 1510.

| 31 BC | 27 BC | 27 BC–AD 14 | AD 14–37 | AD 37–41 | AD 41–54 | AD 54–68 | AD 64 |
|---|---|---|---|---|---|---|---|
| Octavian defeats Antony and Cleopatra at the battle of Actium, and takes control of Egypt. | End of the Republic, start of the Roman empire. | Octavian takes the title Augustus and rules as the first Roman emperor. | Tiberius rules. | Caligula rules. | Claudius rules. | Nero rules. | Fire devastates Rome. |

# Roman Society

THE AMAZING expansion and success of the Roman empire was due largely to its army, which was the best trained and best equipped in the world.

Roman coins bore the head of the emperor and were used in trade all over the empire. Peaceful trading was one of the benefits of Roman rule.

THE ROMAN ARMY was originally formed to protect the city of Rome. It was made up largely of volunteer soldiers. General Marius (155–86 BC) reorganized the army into a more disciplined and efficient fighting force. Soldiers were paid wages and joined up for 20 to 25 years.

Ordinary soldiers were grouped into units called legions, each made up of about 5,000 men. The legions, in turn, were made up of smaller units, called centuries, of 80 men. These were commanded by soldiers called centurions.

Roman soldiers were well trained and well organized. Wearing heavy armour and plumed bronze or iron helmets, they were capable of marching 30 km a day carrying weapons, food and camping kit.

| AD 69–79 | AD 79–81 | C. AD 80 | AD 98–117 | AD 117–138 | AD 166–167 | AD 180 |
|---|---|---|---|---|---|---|
| Vespasian rules the Roman empire. | Titus is emperor. | In Rome, the Colosseum is completed. | Under Emperor Trajan, the empire reaches its greatest extent. | Hadrian rules. | Plague devastates the empire. | End of the *Pax Romana* (Roman Peace), a time of stability in the empire. |

The sight of the legions marching into battle behind their silver standards must have been formidable.

Roman society was divided into citizens and non-citizens. There were three classes of citizens – *patricians,* the richest aristocrats; *equites,* the wealthy merchants; and *plebeians,* the ordinary citizens. All citizens were allowed to vote in elections and to serve in the army. They were also allowed to wear togas.

Emperor Hadrian (ruled AD 117–138) concentrated on strengthening the borders of his already huge empire. Fortified walls were built along vulnerable borders in Germany, Africa and Britain. The best preserved is Hadrian's Wall in Britain, built in AD 122 to defend the empire's northernmost frontier.

The Colosseum is one of the most splendid Roman remains in Rome. It was built to stage gladiator fights, a popular form of entertainment. Gladiators were trained slaves or prisoners, who fought each other, or wild animals, to the death. The Colosseum held up to 45,000 spectators.

Building, mining and all hard manual labour was done by the vast workforce of slaves. Many slaves were treated cruelly, but some were paid a wage and could eventually buy their freedom.

## CHRISTIANITY AND ROME

The Romans worshipped many gods and often adopted new religions from the people they conquered. Jesus Christ was born (probably in 4 BC) in Palestine, then a Roman province. His teachings attracted fervent followers, but upset local Jewish leaders, and he was crucified by the Romans. Christ's followers, among them the apostle Paul, spread the new religion of Christianity throughout the Roman world. Despite persecution, the faith grew and in AD 391 it became the official religion of Rome.

| 286 | AD 391 | AD 410 | AD 451 | AD 476 |
|---|---|---|---|---|
| Emperor Diocletian divides the Roman empire into west and east, each with its own emperor. | Christianity becomes the official religion of the Roman empire. | Rome is captured by Alaric the Visigoth. | Attila the Hun invades Roman Gaul. | The last western emperor, Romulus Augustulus, is deposed. The eastern empire continues as the Byzantine empire. |

# Empires of India

IN ABOUT 321 BC, a young prince, Chandragupta Maurya, founded an empire that stretched across northern India from the Hindu Kush in the west to Bengal in the east. This was the first Indian empire.

◀ In early Buddhist art, Buddha was represented by a symbol such as a footprint, a stupa, a wheel, a lotus flower, or a sacred tree.

## HINDUISM

The Hindu religion began more than 4,000 years ago as ideas from the Indus Valley civilization mingled with those of invading peoples. Under Ashoka, Buddhism became the major religion of India. Hinduism enjoyed a revival under the Guptas. Today, more than three-quarters of Indians are Hindu. The main symbol of Hinduism is the word 'Om' (shown above).

▶ Exquisite wall paintings cover the Buddhist cave temples at Ajanta in western India. The paintings date from the time of the Gupta empire. Some show scenes from the life of the Buddha.

CHANDRAGUPTA'S grandson, Ashoka, came to the throne in 269 BC. He extended the empire until most of India came under Mauryan rule. In 260 BC Ashoka's army fought a bloody battle against the people of Kalinga in eastern India. Sickened by the bloodshed, Ashoka was filled with remorse. He converted to Buddhism and vowed to follow its teachings of peace and non-violence.

Ashoka travelled far and wide throughout his empire, listening to people's views and complaints and trying to improve their lot. He had edicts carved on pillars for people to see, and sent out special officers to explain his policy of religious tolerance, respect for others and peace.

| c. 563 BC | c. 483 BC | c. 321 BC | 269–232 BC | 260 BC | c. 185 BC | c. AD 320 |
|---|---|---|---|---|---|---|
| Birth of the Buddha in Lumbini, Nepal. | Death of the Buddha in Kushinagara, India. | Chandragupta seizes power and founds the Mauryan dynasty. | Reign of Ashoka Maurya, thought by some to be the greatest ruler of ancient India. | Ashoka converts to Buddhism after the battle of Kalinga. | The Shunga dynasty replaces the Mauryans. | The beginnings of Gupta power emerge in the Ganges valley. |

After the collapse of the Mauryan empire in about 185 BC, India was divided into small, independent kingdoms. In AD 320, Chandra Gupta I, ruler of the kingdom of Magadha in the Ganges valley, enlarged his kingdom. The Gupta empire ruled northern India for the next 200 years. Chandra Gupta's son, Samudra, extended the empire and increased its trading links. He was succeeded by Chandra Gupta II. During his reign, India enjoyed a Golden Age.

Under the Guptas, arts and literature flourished, as did science, medicine and mathematics. Great poets and artists were invited to the splendid royal court. Hinduism replaced Buddhism as the major religion of the empire, and many new temples and shrines were built. Sanskrit, the sacred, classical language of India, became the language of the court.

◤ The gateway to the great stupa (Buddhist shrine) of Sanchi, which was built during Ashoka's reign. The first stupas contained relics of the Buddha. Ashoka had stupas built throughout his empire.

◀ Emperor Ashoka Maurya. In Sarnath, where the Buddha first taught, Ashoka erected a tall pillar topped with four lions and four wheels (symbols of Buddhism). It is India's national emblem today.

## BUDDHISM

Buddhism was founded by an Indian prince, Siddharta Gautama (c. 563–483 BC), who gave up his comfortable life to seek enlightenment. He found enlightenment while sitting and meditating under a Bo tree. He spent the rest of his life travelling and teaching. Buddhism teaches that people, like all living things, are part of an endless round of birth, change, death and rebirth. Buddhism spread from India to other parts of Asia, and beyond.

| AD 350–550 | AD 380–415 | C. AD 550 |
|---|---|---|
| The Gupta empire brings a Golden Age of Hinduism to India. | The reign of Chandra Gupta II, greatest of the Gupta kings. | Hun invasions weaken Gupta power. The empire splits into smaller kingdoms. |

# The Middle Ages

## KINGS AND CONFLICTS 500–1400

THE PERIOD FROM about 500 to 1400 in Europe is known as the Middle Ages, or the medieval period. It began with the fall of the Roman empire and ended with the Renaissance, when a revival of art and learning swept through Europe.

THE MEDIEVAL PERIOD was an age of wars and conquests. Some wars were fought to gain more territory, while others were wars of religion, fought between people of differing faiths in an age when religion dominated most people's lives. At this time China's civilization was far in advanc of the rest of the world. Africa and America saw the emergence

| 500s | 529 | 600 | c. 610 | 700 | 732 | 751 | 787 | 800 | 802 |
|---|---|---|---|---|---|---|---|---|---|
| The Eastern Roman empire is at its height. | The first abbey in Europe is Monte Cassino (Italy). | Teotihuacan civilization in Mexico. | The prophet Muhammad begins preaching in Arabia. | The Mayan civilization is at its height. | The battle of Poitiers checks the Muslim advance in Europe. | The Carolingian dynasty is founded. | Vikings begin their attacks on England. | Charlemagne is crowned Holy Roman Emperor. | Founding of the Khmer empire ir Southeas Asia. |

of strong, well-organized empires based on trade, while the spread of Islam from Arabia across the Middle East and into North Africa and Spain brought a new way of life to a vast area.

During the Middle Ages, ordinary people lived simply, as farmers in villages or as craftworkers in towns. Many built their own houses, made their own clothes and grew their own food. Poor people obeyed local landowners or lords, who in turn served a more powerful king or emperor. The rulers ordered castles and palaces, temples and cathedrals to

be built. These huge stone buildings often took many years, and even centuries, to construct.

Few people travelled far from their homes. Those who did venture into foreign lands included merchants, soldiers and a few bold explorers who wrote accounts of their travels. Few people could read or write, and learning was passed down by word of mouth. In Europe, the monasteries were centres of learning, while in Asia the Chinese and Arabs led the way in science and technology, medicine and astronomy.

| 900 | c. 1000 | 1066 | 1096–1270 | 1150 | 1206 | 1271 | 1300s | 1325 | 1348–1349 |
|---|---|---|---|---|---|---|---|---|---|
| Rise of the Toltecs in Mexico and Ghana's empire in Africa. | Vikings land in North America. | The Norman conquest of England. | Eight Crusades to the Holy Land. | The temple of Angkor Wat in Cambodia is completed. | Genghis Khan rules the Mongols. | Marco Polo travels to China from Venice. | Long period of civil wars in Japan. | Aztecs found Tenochtitlan. | Black Death ravages Europe. |

# Byzantium

FOR OVER 500 years the Roman empire brought a unique way of life to a vast area of land. But in 476 the western half of the empire collapsed, overrun by invading German tribes. In the east, Roman rule continued to flourish under what is called the Byzantine empire.

⌃ The magnificent church of Hagia Sophia in Istanbul was completed in 537. It took only six years to build. The minarets were added later when it became a mosque. It is now a museum.

THE OLD GREEK city-port of Byzantium (modern-day Istanbul in Turkey) was the centre of the Byzantine (Eastern Roman) empire. Renamed Constantinople after the first Byzantine emperor, Constantine, it became the seat of the Byzantine emperors and the centre of the eastern Christian Church. Within the Byzantine empire, Greek and Roman arts and learning were preserved. Byzantine churches, such as Hagia Sophia, contained detailed frescoes and mosaic pictures made from hundreds of pieces of glass or stone.

The Byzantine empire reached its peak in the 500s, under the emperor Justinian and his general Belisarius. It included Italy, Greece, Turkey, parts of Spain, North Africa and Egypt.

▷ Constantine the Great (275–337) was the first Christian emperor of Rome. He moved the empire's capital from Rome to Byzantium and renamed the city Constantinople.

▷ Chariot races mixed thrills with politics. Howling mobs in the Hippodrome cheered for the Blues or the Greens, in support of one or other of the rival political factions.

| 330 | 408 | 445 | 476 | c. 501 | 527–565 | 678 |
|---|---|---|---|---|---|---|
| Constantinople is founded. | Emperor Theodosius begins building a great wall to protect Constantinople. | Attila the Hun attacks. He is paid to go away. | Fall of the Western Roman empire. | A long series of wars with Persia begins. | Reign of Justinian I. | An Arab siege of Constantinople is defeated. |

Justinian's powerful wife, Theodora, helped him govern. Justinian issued a code of laws on which the legal systems of many European countries were later based. Constantinople was a busy port and meeting place for traders from as far away as Spain, China and Russia. But invaders from the east – Avars, Slavs and Bulgars – threatened this last Roman empire. After Justinian's death in 565, Byzantium was weakened by many wars and eventually fell to the Turks in 1453.

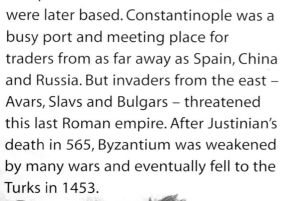

◀ This map shows the Byzantine (Eastern Roman) empire at its height in the 500s. It extended from the eastern Mediterranean to Spain in the west.

▶ In the 6th century, Byzantine artists in a church in Ravenna, Italy, made this mosaic of the Magi (Wise Men) visiting Jesus.

| 900s | 1054 | 1081 | 1200 | 1204 | 1341–1354 | 1453 |
|---|---|---|---|---|---|---|
| Second Golden Age. The Balkans and Russia come under Byzantine influence. | The Christian Church in Constantinople breaks with the Church in Rome. | Alexius I Comnenus seizes power and reforms government. | The Byzantine empire begins to break up under attacks from Turks and Bulgarians. | Constantinople is sacked by Crusaders. | Civil war in the Byzantine empire. | Turks capture Constantinople – end of the Byzantine empire. |

# The Franks

THE FRANKS were the strongest of all the western European peoples who struggled for land and power after the end of the Roman empire in 476.

UNDER THEIR first great leader, Clovis, the Franks spread out from their homeland around the river Rhine (in what is now Germany). They fought their neighbours, such as the Visigoths and Burgundians, until by 540 they had conquered most of the old Roman province of Gaul (modern France, which is named after the Franks).

Clovis defeated rival chieftains to bring all the Frankish tribes under his control. His family became known as the Merovingian dynasty, after his grandfather Merovich. Clovis became a Christian and ruled from Paris, governing his lands through Church bishops and nobles. The nobles or lords held estates known as manors, which were ploughed and farmed by peasants.

Frankish leaders were always ready to defend their estates and conquer new lands. Their eagerness to ride into battle meant they needed servants for military service. In return, the servants were granted land. This was the beginning of feudalism. Leading families jockeyed for the king's favour. In the 600s two rival clans

◄ An ivory carving shows Gregory the Great, pope from 590 to 604. From the time of Clovis, the Franks were Christian.

▲ Examples of fine metalwork from the Frankish period. These gold and enamel buckles date from the 6th to 7th centuries and would have been worn by a rich noble.

| 241 | 350 | 428 | 451 | c. 466 | 486 |
|---|---|---|---|---|---|
| First mention of Franks, fighting the future Roman emperor Aurelian in Mainz. | Franks are brought under Roman rule. | Salian Franks (living in the Netherlands and lower Rhineland) throw off Roman rule and invade Gaul, led by King Chlodio. | Franks join with Romans to defeat Attila the Hun at the battle of Châlons. | Clovis is born. In 481 he becomes king of the Franks. | Franks defeat the last great Roman army in the West, at the battle of Soissons. |

◀ The Franks were farmers. They tilled their fields in strips using wheeled ploughs pulled by oxen. Oxen were slower than horses, but stronger.

▶ A Frankish stone monument, possibly a gravestone. The carving shows a warrior with a long broadsword, a favourite weapon of the Franks.

🔽 Tough Frankish warriors rode into battle with shaven heads and topknots, wearing light mail armour. They were formidable cavalry fighters, whose loyalty was rewarded with booty. Frankish armies defeated the Romans, Gauls and Visigoths who tried to halt their expansion.

fought for power. The Austrasians ousted the Neustrians, and their chief, Pepin of Herstal, founded a new ruling family. Pepin's son, Charles Martel (known as the Hammer), won an historic battle at Poitiers against Muslim invaders in 732. This defeat checked the advance of Islam into central Europe. Martel's son, Pepin the Short, established the new Carolingian dynasty. He was the first Frankish king anointed by the pope, in 754. But the greatest of the Frankish rulers was Pepin's son, Charlemagne.

| 496 | 506 | 511 | 540 | 687 | 732 | 751 |
|---|---|---|---|---|---|---|
| Clovis defeats the Alemanni near the river Seine. | Franks defeat the Visigoths. | Clovis dies. | Franks control most of Gaul and lands in what is now Germany. | After the battle of Tertry, Pepin of Herstal becomes the most powerful Frankish leader. | Charles Martel defeats a Muslim army at the battle of Poitiers. | Last Merovingian king, Childeric III, is overthrown. Pepin the Short (Charlemagne's father) becomes king. |

# The Rise of Islam

THE NEW FAITH preached by the prophet Muhammad in the 600s changed the course of history. Muhammad's followers spread their religion, Islam, by preaching and conquest. By the 700s, Muslims (followers of Islam) ruled most of the Middle East and North Africa.

The Dome of the Rock in Jerusalem. Muslims believe Muhammad ascended to heaven from the rock to speak with God, before returning to Earth to spread Islam.

BEFORE MUHAMMAD, the Arab peoples were not united in any way. Different groups worshipped different gods. Muhammad was a merchant of Mecca, in Arabia. At the age of about 40 he began to preach of belief in one God, after a dream in which an angel told him he was the prophet of Allah (God). The new religion became Islam, which means "submission to the will of Allah".

Muhammad had to leave Mecca when some townspeople objected to his new teaching. His journey in 622 to Yathrib (now Medina) is commemorated still as the Hegira, which begins the Muslim calendar. In Medina, Muhammad and his followers built the first mosque. His teachings and revelations were written down in the Koran, the holy book of Islam. In 630 Muhammad's followers captured Mecca, and Islam became the new religion of Arabia.

A Muslim star-chart of a constellation. Muslim astronomers studied the stars and preserved many older Greek ideas about the universe.

| 570 | 610 | 622 | 625 | 630 | 632 | 634 | 644 |
|---|---|---|---|---|---|---|---|
| Probable birth date of Muhammad. | Muhammad begins preaching in Mecca. | Muhammad's flight to Yathrib (now Medina). | Muhammad's teachings are written down in the Koran. | Muhammad leads an army into Mecca. | Muhammad dies. Abu Bakr becomes the first caliph. | Omar succeeds Abu Bakr. | Othman (head of the Ummayads) succeeds Omar. |

SPAIN 711–713
CARTHAGE 687–688
SYRIA 638
ARABIA 632
PERSIA 644
MEDITERRANEAN SEA
Cairo
Medina
Mecca
MAURETANIA 700–705
BARCA 643
EGYPT 639–643
BABYLONIA 637
INDIAN OCEAN

◄ This map shows how rapidly the new religion of Islam spread from Arabia as far west as Spain.

١ ٢ ٣ ٤ ٥ ٦ ٧ ٨ ٩ ١٠ ٠

1 2 3 4 5 6 7 8 9 10 0

▲ Arabic numerals (bottom row) evolved from Hindu numbers (top) through trade with India. They proved easier to use than Roman numerals.

When Muhammad died in 632, his father-in-law, Abu Bakr, was chosen as first caliph (successor). A group called the Shiites thought only the descendants of Muhammad's daughter Fatima could lead Islam. Others, known as Sunnis, thought any Muslim could do so. This split continues today.

By 644 the Arabs had conquered most of Syria, Palestine and Persia. After 661, the Ummayad family controlled the growing empire from their capital, Damascus, in Syria. Islam's advance into Europe was halted by the Frankish army of Charles Martel in 732. In 762 the new Abbasid dynasty moved the empire's capital to Baghdad (in what is now Iraq). This city became the centre of the Islamic world.

◄ Mecca is the city in Saudi Arabia to which Muslims turn when they pray and to which millions of pilgrims travel. Pilgrims circle the shrine containing the Black Stone, believed by Muslims to have been given to Abraham by the angel Gabriel.

▶ Harun al-Rashid (766–806) was caliph from 786. The power of the Abbasid dynasty of caliphs peaked during his reign.

| 556 | 661 | 732 | 750 | 756 |
|---|---|---|---|---|
| The Shiite leader Ali becomes caliph. | The Islamic capital is moved from Mecca to Damascus. | Abd-al-Rahman, ruler of Spain, invades France. He is defeated by a Frankish army led by Charles Martel. | Abbasid dynasty is founded by Abu al-Abbas. | Last Ummayad ruler flees from Damascus to Cordoba, Spain. |

# The Maya

THE MAYA lived in Central America. Their civilization lasted more than 700 years. They built huge cities with magnificent stone temples that can still be seen today.

A Mayan calendar. The Mayan number system was based on 20. The farmers' calendar had 18 months of 20 days each.

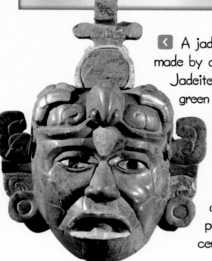

A jadeite mask made by a Mayan artist. Jadeite is a hard, green gemstone. Much of Mayan art was religious. This mask may have been used by a priest during a ceremony.

to grow beans, corn and squash. They raised turkeys and kept bees, but had no domestic animals other than dogs. The only wheeled vehicles were toy carts.

The largest Mayan city was Tikal, in what is now Guatemala, with a population of 60,000. Crowds filled the large squares around the pyramid-

THE MAYA were at their most powerful from about 200 to 900, although their culture lasted until the Spanish conquest of Central America in the early 1500s. They lived in well-organized city-states, each with its own ruler. The rulers fought wars with neighbouring city-states. They also controlled trade in obsidian, cacao, cotton and other goods such as colourful feathers, used to make headdresses. In the countryside farmers cleared forest land and terraced the hillsides

**3372 BC**
First date in Mayan calendar.

**400 BC**
The Maya have built several large pyramid-temples, like those at Tikal in Guatemala.

**AD 250**
Start of the classic period of Mayan civilization. The Maya borrow some of their ideas from the people of Teotihuacan.

The Maya settled in what is now eastern Mexico. There were some 50 states, each with its own ruler and sacred city, such as Chichén Itzá, Tikal and Copán.

temples to watch ceremonies conducted by priests, who studied the heavens to predict eclipses of the Moon and Sun. Religion was important to the Maya. They made sacrifices to win favours from their many gods. Mostly they sacrificed animals, but they also threw human victims into sacred wells. The Maya invented the first writing in America. They wrote codexes (folding books) on pages of tree bark, three of which survive. They also set up tall carved stones to commemorate dates and important events. Many people in Mexico still speak Mayan languages.

A Mayan ruler enters his city. Each city-ruler was a god-king. Everyone worshipped him and offered tribute in the form of goods, food or work.

| . 700 | c. 900 | 900 | 990 | c. 1250 | 1440 | 1517 |
|---|---|---|---|---|---|---|
| Mayan cities each reatest rosperity. | Decline of Mayan civilization. People move to the highlands of Mexico and Guatemala. | Chichén Itzá is the most important Mayan city. It is governed by a council. | Toltec people take over Chichén Itzá. | Mayan culture revives: Mayapán is the chief city. | Rebellion against Mayapán rulers. Maya unity weakened as states fight one another. | Start of Spanish conquest of Maya lands. |

48

# Charlemagne

CHARLES I, king of the Franks, was known as Charlemagne (Charles the Great). He founded the Holy Roman empire in Europe and was long regarded by many people as the "ideal ruler".

CHARLEMAGNE was born in 742. His father was King Pepin, son of the famous soldier Charles Martel, and founder of the new Frankish ruling family (later called the Carolingian dynasty, after the Latin name for Charlemagne). In 768 Pepin died, leaving his kingdom to his sons Carloman and Charlemagne. Carloman soon died, and Charlemagne was left in sole control.

A very tall man, convinced of his own destiny, Charlemagne had learned much from his ruthless warrior father. He led his armies out of the Frankish homeland of France into what are now the Netherlands, Germany and Italy. Wherever he conquered non-Christians, such as the Saxons of Germany and the Avars of Hungary, he forced them to become Christians and to take part in mass baptisms.

There was more to Charlemagne than simply waging wars of conquest. He learned to read Latin and greatly admired scholarship. His capital at

| 742 | 768 | 771 | 772 | 774 | 778 |
|---|---|---|---|---|---|
| Probable birth date of Charlemagne. | Pepin the Short (Charlemagne's father) dies. | Charlemagne becomes ruler of the Franks. | Charlemagne starts war with Saxons and converts them to Christianity. | Charlemagne makes Lombardy (Italy) part of his empire. | Charlemagne fights the Muslims in Spain. His army is attacked by the Basques at the battle of Roncesvalles. |

NORTH SEA

BRITISH ISLES

SAXONS

Aachen

AUSTRASIA

THURINGIA

BOHEMIA

BRITTANY

Paris

NEUSTRIA

Strasbourg

BAVARIA

AVARS

ATLANTIC OCEAN

BURGUNDY

CARINTHIA

AQUITAINE

LOMBARDY

PROVENCE

Roncesvalles

TUSCANY

SPAIN

CORSICA

Rome

ADRIATIC SEA

MEDITERRANEAN SEA

◀ Charlemagne's empire grew from the lands of Austrasia (France and Germany) he inherited from his father Pepin in 768 and his brother in 771 (in orange on the map). The Frankish empire was at its biggest extent soon after (orange and red).

Charlemagne's position as Europe's strongest leader was recognized in 800 when the pope crowned him Holy Roman emperor. After he died in 814 the Holy Roman empire, weakened by attacks, was soon split between his three grandsons. It survived, however, in one form or another until 1806.

Aachen was the glittering centre of his empire, with a splendid palace and heated swimming pool. But the emperor himself dressed and lived simply. He had books read aloud to him and invited to his court famous scholars such as Alcuin of York.

After Charlemagne's death many stories were written about him. A skirmish during his Spanish campaign of 778 became the subject of the medieval epic poem *The Song of Roland*.

◀ The tomb of Charlemagne at the imperial capital, Aachen, dates from 1215. It is decorated with gold and precious stones. Artists working 400 years after Charlemagne's death were able to refer to written descriptions of his appearance, but had no likeness of him to copy.

▶ The iron lance of the Holy Roman emperors was a holy relic as well as a symbol of power. Around the spearpoint is a gold sheath stretched over a nail reputedly from Christ's cross.

**800**
Charlemagne is crowned Emperor of the West by Pope Leo III.

rs with Lombards, arians, Avars, tons and others.

**804**
Last of 18 campaigns against the Saxons.

**808**
Charlemagne fights the Danes.

**814**
Charlemagne dies. His son Louis the Pious succeeds.

**817**
The empire is split between Louis's sons.

50

# The Vikings

THE VIKINGS were great explorers. They set sail from Scandinavia (Norway, Sweden and Denmark) looking for new lands, and reached Greenland, Britain and the Mediterranean and Black seas. Not all came as raiders; many were peaceful farmers and traders.

Wooden bucket

Leather shoe

Iron knife

Pottery dish

Carved stone

Antler skate

Viking farmers made tools, clothes, furnitu and things to sell at market. Wood, ivory, deer antler, leather, clay, bone and iron were commor materials used.

SCANDINAVIA, the homeland of the Vikings, was covered in mountains and forests, and had little good farmland. Most Vikings lived close to the sea, tending small fields where they grew rye, barley, wheat and oats, and vegetables such as turnips and carrots. They kept cattle and sheep, and caught fish in the rivers and fiords. Traders travelled on horseback or by boat to

Many Vikings lived on small farms, often near to rivers or the sea. They planted cereals and vegetables, and kept pigs, cows, goats and sheep. Women wore linen dresses with wool tunics on top, fastened by brooches.

| Late 700s | 841 | 850 | c. 860 | c. 861 | 862 | 874 | 900s |
|---|---|---|---|---|---|---|---|
| The trading town of Hedeby in Denmark is founded. | Vikings found Dublin on Ireland's east coast. | Probable date of the Oseberg ship burial in Oslo Fiord, Norway – the richest Viking ship burial found. | Vikings settle around the Baltic. They rule Novgorod in Russia. | Ingolf is the first Viking to reach Iceland. | The Slavs and Finns of north Russia invite the Vikings to rule. | First Viking settlers reach Iceland. | Viking traders visit Constantinople which they call Miklagaard. |

## THE THING

The Viking law court was called the Thing. Every year local people came together for several days, and any freeman who had a complaint or an argument to settle could raise the matter. His neighbours would listen and give a judgement. A person refusing to obey the Thing's verdict became an outlaw, to be killed on sight.

market towns such as Hedeby in Denmark to exchange furs, reindeer antlers and walrus ivory for weapons, jewels and pottery.

Viking families lived in houses made of wood, stone or turf. Smoke from the cooking fire found its way out through a hole in the roof.

Around the fire people sat at benches and tables to eat hearty meals, play dice games and tell stories. The Vikings loved stories, especially those about their heroes and gods. The most important god of Norse (Scandinavian) mythology was Odin, the wise and one-eyed, but the most popular was Thor, the thunder god, whose symbol was a hammer. Physical sports such as wrestling, horse fights and ice skating were also popular.

Viking farmers often had thralls (slaves) to help with the work, but most men were karls (freemen). A rich jarl, or landowner, was expected to share his wealth with his followers, feasting and entertaining them in his great hall. Powerful jarls became Viking chiefs. As the population increased, farmland became increasingly scarce. From the late 700s, these Viking chiefs and their warriors began to venture from their homelands in search of better farmland and greater riches.

| 960 | 982 | c. 1000 | 1000 | 1030 | 1100s |
|---|---|---|---|---|---|
| King Harald Bluetooth of Denmark becomes a Christian. | Erik the Red reaches Greenland and founds a settlement. | Erik's son Leif Eriksson reaches Vinland (North America). | Jorvik (York), England has a population of 10,000 people. | By King Olaf the Holy's reign, Norway is Christian. | The Swedes are the last Vikings to give up their old religion and convert to Christianity. |

# The Crusades

FOR European Christians, the Crusades were holy wars, with the promise of plunder in the service of the Church. For more than 200 years, Christian and Muslim armies fought for control of the Holy Land, the territory around Jerusalem in the Middle East.

KEY
— First Crusade
— Second Crusade
— Third Crusade

The journey to the Holy Land was long. Crusaders endured sickness, thirst and attack as they struggled over rough, often desert, terrain.

**Catapults threw flaming tar and rocks**

**Round towers gave defenders better angles for arrows**

MANY CHRISTIAN pilgrims visited Jerusalem, which was a holy city to Jews and Muslims, as well as to Christians. But Jerusalem was held by Muslim Turks, and in 1095 they banned Christian pilgrims from the city. This angered both the western Christian Church, based in Rome, and the eastern Christian Church in Constantinople. From Rome, Pope Urban II called on Christians to free Jerusalem, and so launched the First Crusade, or war of the cross. In 1096 a European force joined with an army from Constantinople. Their leaders were

Both sides built strong castles. To capture a castle, soldiers besieged it, sometimes for months. They battered at the gates and tried to blow up the walls, while being bombarded with missiles from inside.

| 1096 | 1099 | 1147 | 1187 | 1189 | 1191 | 1202 |
|---|---|---|---|---|---|---|
| First Crusade, called by Pope Urban II. Peter the Hermit leads a peasant army across Europe. | Crusaders defeat the Turks and capture Jerusalem. | Second Crusade. German and French armies are beaten. | Saladin captures Jerusalem. | Third Crusade, led by Frederick I Barbarossa of the Holy Roman empire, Philip II of France and Richard I of England. | Crusaders capture the port of Acre in Palestine. | Fourth Crusade attacks Egypt. |

Saladin (1138–1193) was the greatest of the Muslim leaders. He took Jerusalem, but in 1192 made peace with Richard I, allowing Christian pilgrims to enter the city.

inspired by religious faith, but also by a desire to increase territory and wealth. In three years they captured Jerusalem and went on to set up Christian kingdoms in Palestine. None of the seven later crusades matched this success.

The Crusades inspired many stories of bravery and honour on both sides. But

Crusaders found the weather in the Holy Land very hot, and soon learned from Muslim soldiers that it was best to wear airy, loose robes over their armour.

CHILDREN'S CRUSADE OF 1212
Inspired by two boy preachers, 50,000 children in two groups, one from France and one from Germany, set off for the Holy Land. Some died on the journey, and many others were sold as slaves in North Africa.

disasters also happened. Before the First Crusade even set out, a peasant army known as the People's Crusade wandered across Europe and was eventually massacred by the Turks. Then the Fourth Crusade of 1202 turned aside to loot the Christian city of Constantinople.

The Crusaders never did win back the Holy Land. But Europeans learned more about Eastern science, food and medicine as trade between Europe and Asia grew.

Transport ships were loaded with soldiers and equipment bound for the Crusades. Groups of knights, including the powerful Knights Templars, protected journeying Christians.

| 04 | 1221 | 1228 | 1244 | 1249 | 1270 | 1291 |
|---|---|---|---|---|---|---|
| usaders capture onstantinople. | Fifth Crusade. Crusaders fight the Sultan of Egypt. | The Sixth Crusade ends when Muslims hand over Jerusalem. | Muslims retake Jerusalem. | Seventh Crusade is led by Louis IX of France. | Eighth Crusade also led by Louis. He and many of his men die of plague in Tunis. | Acre, last crusader stronghold, is captured. |

# A Medieval Town

IN THE Middle Ages, towns in Europe were noisy and crowded by day, but quiet and dark at night. The silence was broken only by watchmen calling out the hours. Churches, guilds, fairs and markets all drew people into the towns.

▷ This medieval painting shows French tradesmen at work in their shops. Tailors stitch richly coloured cloth and a grocer sets out his goods. Up the street a barber is shaving a customer.

IF YOU WALKED through a medieval town, you took care where you stepped, because people threw out their rubbish into the muddy streets. Open drains ran alongside and smelled foul. People either fetched water from the town well or bought it from the water-seller, hoping it was

clean. Pigs and chickens wandered in and out of small yards. Houses were built close together, with the top floors often jutting out over the streets. Since most houses were made chiefly of wood, they caught fire easily. At night, the curfew bell warned people to cover or put out their kitchen fires.

Many houses doubled as workshops and shops. Craftworkers and traders formed groups

◁ Stained-glass windows told stories in pictures. In church, people who could not read looked at the colourful Bible stories to learn more about the Christian faith.

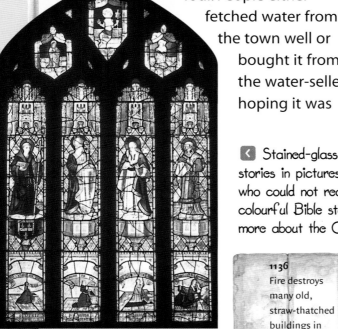

| 1136 | 1162 | 1200s | 1209 |
|---|---|---|---|
| Fire destroys many old, straw-thatched buildings in London. | Work begins on the cathedral of Notre Dame in Paris, which by 1210 is a city with paved streets, walls and twenty-four gates. | Many new towns are founded in Europe. City-states develop in Italy and Germany. | A new London Bridge is built. |

## MONEY MAKES MONEY

European merchants usually carried silver coins, but Arabs preferred gold. As international trade increased, Italian merchants set up the first banks, using written bills of exchange to pay for goods instead of heavy bags of coins.

called guilds to organize their businesses and to set standards of work. Guilds also staged pageants and plays in the streets. Some towns were famous for their fairs, which attracted merchants from all over Europe, as well as entertainers, fake doctors and pickpockets.

In towns, work was to be found building magnificent cathedrals, churches and defensive walls. Large trading cities in Europe, such as Hamburg, Antwerp and London, grew rich from buying and selling wool and other goods. About 90 cities in northern Europe formed the Hanseatic League to fight pirates, win more trade and keep out rivals.

Market day in a medieval town. People brought in farm produce to sell, visited stalls and shops, gossiped and drank at the ale house. Acrobats, actors and dancing bears amused the crowds.

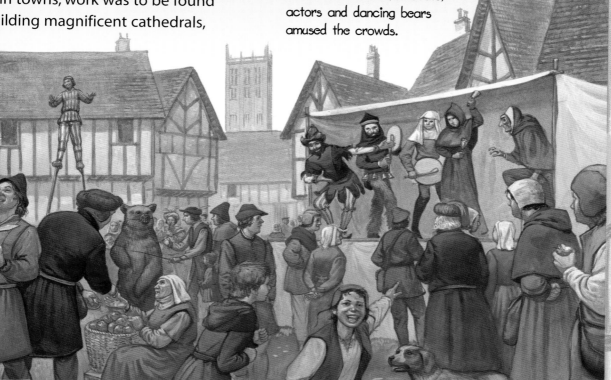

| 260 | 1285 | 1300 | 1348–1349 | 1377 | 1400s |
|---|---|---|---|---|---|
| he German towns f Lubeck and amburg form a ade association, ter known as the anseatic League. | English merchants are banned from selling their goods in churchyards. | The wool trade is at its peak in England. Large churches are built in prosperous wool towns. | People flee towns during the Black Death in England. | London by now has at least 50 guilds and a population of more than 35,000. | Morality plays, in which actors stage tales of good against evil, are performed in churches or in the streets. |

# The Mongol Empire

"**I**NHUMAN and beastly, rather monsters than men..." is how the English historian Matthew Paris described the Mongols in the 1200s. Mongol armies sent a shockwave of fear around Asia and Europe, conquering a vast area of land that formed the largest empire in history.

▶ Genghis Khan's empire extended from the river Danube in the west to the Pacific in the east. The capital was Karakorum.

THE MONGOLS lived on the plains of Central Asia, from the Ural mountains to the Gobi Desert. They were nomads, wandering with their herds and living in portable tents (yurts). Their leaders were called khans. In 1206, Temujin Khan brought all the tribes under his rule and was proclaimed Genghis Khan, "lord of all". In a lifetime of conquest, he seized an empire that extended from the Pacific Ocean to the river Danube, incorporating the Persian empire.

▶ Mongols preferred to fight on horseback. Warriors controlled their horses with their feet, leaving their hands free to shoot bows and hurl spears. Mongol cavalry charges usually overwhelmed the enemy.

| 1206 | 1211 | 1215 | 1217 | 1219 | 1224 |
|---|---|---|---|---|---|
| Temujin is chosen to be khan of all the Mongols He takes the name Genghis Khan. | The Mongol army attacks China. | Beijing, capital of China, is taken by the Mongols. | China and Korea are controlled by the Mongols. Their new capital is Karakorum. | The Mongols sweep west to attack the empire of Khwarezm (Persia and Turkey). | Mongol armies invade Russia, then Poland and Hungary. |

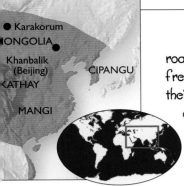

Karakorum
MONGOLIA
Khanbalik
(Beijing)
CIPANGU
KATHAY
MANGI

> The Mongols roamed in search of fresh grassland for their sheep, horses and goats. They carried their felt houses (yurts) with them on ox carts.

The Mongols continued their attacks after Genghis Khan died. In 1237 a Mongol army led by Batu Khan, one of Genghis's sons, invaded Russia.

In Europe, people panicked as word spread of the Mongols' speed and ferocity in battle. Mongol soldiers travelled with five horses each and were expert with bows and lances. In victory, they were merciless, slaughtering the people of a city and carting away treasure. Western Europe was saved only when the Mongols turned homeward on the death of their leader Ogadai Khan in 1241.

> Genghis Khan was ruthless in battle, but kept peace in his empire and ruled fairly, if sternly. Trade flourished during his rule.

MARES' MILK
Horses were vital to the Mongols, who drank fresh mares' milk. They also fermented the milk in skin bags hung from wooden frames to make a strong drink called kumiss. At victory celebrations, kumiss was drunk and fiddles strung with horsehair were played.

| 1227 | 1237 | 1241 |
|---|---|---|
| Genghis Khan dies. In 1229 his son Ogadai is chosen as the new khan. | Mongol generals Batu and Subotai invade northern Russia. Their army is known as the Golden Horde. | Ogadai dies. His armies pull back from Europe. |

# The Black Death

THE Black Death was the most horrific natural disaster of the Middle Ages. It was a devastating plague that killed many millions of people in Europe and Asia. One Italian historian wrote: "This is the end of the world".

THE PLAGUE came to Europe from Asia 1347. Disease ravaged a Mongol army fighting in the Crimea (southern Russia). The desperate Mongols catapulted diseased corpses over the walls of a fortress defended by Italians. When the Italians sailed home to Genoa, they carried the disease with them.

The disease was bubonic plague, passed to humans from infected rats through flea bites. The name

| 1344 | 1347 | 1348 | 1349 | 1350 | 1353 |
|---|---|---|---|---|---|
| Bubonic plague breaks out in China and India. | The plague reaches Genoa in Italy and spreads west. | In the summer, the disease hits southern England. In the winter, it reaches London. | The Black Death spreads to Ireland, Wales and Scotland. Also affected are France, Spain, Germany and Russia. | The epidemic reaches Scandinavia. | The Black Death epidemic eases. As many as 25 million people in Europe are dead. |

A picture of the time shows a procession of penitents whipping themselves in the streets.

The Black Death raged from China to Scandinavia. As it spread, panic-stricken people fled from the towns. Wherever they went, the plague went with them. So many people died (at least 25 million, or a third of the people in Europe) that villages were left deserted and fields overgrown. The Church lost many priests, the only educated men of the time. Half of England's monks and nuns died, and three archbishops of Canterbury died in one year.

"Black Death" came from the black spots that appeared on victims, who also developed swellings in their armpits and groin, and coughed up blood. Many people died the same day they fell ill. No medieval doctor knew why the Black Death struck or how to cure it. To many Christians it seemed a punishment from God, and some took to the streets, whipping themselves as a penance for the sins of humanity.

Repeated plague attacks throughout the 14th century left Europe short of people to work and farm the land, and pushed up wages. Unrest over wages and taxes led to an uprising in France in 1358 and to the Peasants' Revolt in England, led by Wat Tyler, in 1381.

Neither town governments nor local doctors could fight the plague. Many people fled, leaving the sick to die. Crosses on doors showed the disease had struck. Carts carried the dead away.

### BLACK DEATH

The black rat carried the fleas that transmitted the disease. The rats travelled on ships from port to port, and as they moved the Black Death spread at terrifying speed. There were rats and fleas in every medieval town and in most houses. Rubbish in the streets and poor sanitation made towns an ideal breeding ground for disease. Many towns lost half their population to the plague, and some villages were abandoned.

| 1358 | 1381 | 1400 |
|---|---|---|
| A peasants' uprising in northern France is savagely put down. | The Peasants' Revolt in England, with rioting in the southeast (in Essex and Kent). | Further outbreaks of the Black Death continue until this date. |

# The Age of Discovery

## EXPLORERS AND EMPIRES 1400–1700

THE 1400s mark the end of the Middle Ages. In Europe, the new ideas of the Renaissance and Reformation transformed the way people thought about themselves and the world, and the way they lived.

THREE EVENTS are often picked out as marking the end of the medieval period and the start of the modern age. They are the fall of Constantinople in 1453, which ended the last traces of the old Roman empire; the development of printing in the 1450s, which made books cheaper and more widely available; and the first voyage of Christopher Columbus to the Americas in 1492.

| 1464 | 1492 | 1497 | 1500 | 1501 | 1517 | 1522 | 1526 | 1535 | 1543 |
|------|------|------|------|------|------|------|------|------|------|
| Rise of Songhai empire in Africa. | Columbus sails from Spain to America. | Portuguese explorers sail to India. | Renaissance is at its height in Italy. | Start of Safavid dynasty in Persia. | Martin Luther begins the Reformation in Europe. | First round-the-world voyage by Magellan's expedition. | Babur founds the Mughal empire in India. | Spain completes conquest of Aztec and Inca empires. | Copernicus argues that the Sun, not the Earth, is centre of the solar system. |

The "Age of Discovery" was a time when the peoples of the world came into increasing contact with each other. People in America, Africa and Asia had greater contact with Europe. Europeans increased their power in the world through trade, through the use of new technology such as cannon and muskets, and through a restless search for new lands and wealth that sent explorers and adventurers across the oceans. By the 1600s, several European countries had established permanent colonies overseas.

This period also saw many new ideas and challenges to old beliefs. Religious quarrels led to bitter wars. There were power struggles between kings and parliaments, as democratic government slowly developed. From the 1500s, there were startling advances in science, with inventions such as the telescope and microscope revealing new wonders, and prompting new questions. Great scientists such as Copernicus, Galileo and Newton challenged the old ideas, and a new freedom of thought began to shake the foundations of society.

| 71 | 1588 | 1590 | 1616 | 1609 | 1618 | 1620 | 1642 | 1643 | 1665 |
|---|---|---|---|---|---|---|---|---|---|
| the battle of panto, ropean hristians defeat uslim Ottoman rks. | Spanish Armada fails to invade England. | Japan is united by Hideyoshi. | First known European landing in Australia. | Galileo uses a telescope to study the stars and planets. | Thirty Years' War begins. | Mayflower pilgrims from England land in America. | English Civil War begins. | Louis XIV becomes king of France. | Isaac Newton reveals the nature of light. |

# The Renaissance

THE RENAISSANCE was a "rebirth" of interest in the art and learning of ancient Greece and Rome. Many historians say that it marked the end of the Middle Ages and the beginning of our modern world. It began in Italy, and in the 1400s spread throughout Europe, changing the way people thought about the world.

THE RENAISSANCE began among the scholars, artists and scientists of Italy. They had new ideas, but also turned to the past, rediscovering the learning of ancient Greece and Rome. Many old handwritten books were brought to Italy by scholars fleeing from the city of Constantinople (the ancient capital of the Eastern Roman empire), which was captured by the Ottoman Turks in 1453. With a greater knowledge of ancient science and beliefs, European schola were inspired to think again about established religious teaching. In literature, great Italian poets such as Petrarch began to explore human emotions. By the early 1500s, three painters of genius – Leonardo da Vinci, Michelangelo and Raphael – were bringing a new energy and realism to

A print workshop in Denmark, about 1600. The technology of printing with a screw press and metal type spread throughout Europe, and for the first time books became widely available.

| 1306 | 1308 | 1387 | 1416 | 1453 | 1454 |
|------|------|------|------|------|------|
| Italian artist Giotto di Bondone paints frescos that are more life-like than earlier medieval paintings. | Dante Alighieri begins writing *The Divine Comedy* in his native Italian, not Latin. | Geoffrey Chaucer begins *The Canterbury Tales*, written in English. | Italian sculptor Donatello breaks new ground with free-standing figures, including his nude *David*. | Constantinople is captured by the Turks; many of its scholars flee to Italy. | Johannes Gutenberg perfects printing with movable type. By 1476 William Caxton is printing in London. |

The new universe, as conceived by Polish astronomer Copernicus in 1543. He put the Sun, not the Earth, at the centre of the universe. This challenged the established theory of the 2nd-century Greek astronomer Ptolemy.

The great dome of Florence Cathedral in Italy, designed by Filippo Brunelleschi, the first major architect of the Italian Renaissance. Begun in 1420, it took 14 years to complete.

art. Architects designed new and elegant buildings that echoed the classical styles of ancient Greece and Rome.

The Renaissance was fuelled by new technology. Printing with movable type, developed by Johannes Gutenberg in Germany, made books cheaper and more plentiful, so new ideas could be read by more people. Some new ideas were astounding, such as Copernicus's theory that the Sun was the centre of the solar system. The Renaissance changed the Western world forever.

A flying machine drawn by the Italian artist Leonardo da Vinci. As well as being an artistic genius, Leonardo was a visionary, devising several futuristic machines.

Dante Alighieri, whose poem *"The Divine Comedy"* explores love, death and faith. Dante wrote in his own language, Italian, and not Latin, which was the language of scholars.

| 1466–1536 | 1478 | 1508 | 1513 | 1516 | 1543 | 1590 |
|---|---|---|---|---|---|---|
| Life of Erasmus. He publishes studies of the Old and New Testaments. | Lorenzo de Medici makes Florence a centre of art and learning. Sandro Botticelli paints *Primavera*. | Michelangelo paints the ceiling of the Sistine Chapel in the Vatican, Rome. | Italian Niccolo Machiavelli writes *The Prince*, on the theory of government. | Sir Thomas More publishes *Utopia*. | Nicolas Copernicus's theory about the solar system. | William Shakespeare is writing plays in England. |

# The Aztecs

THE AZTECS were fierce warriors. They conquered an empire that eventually extended right across Mexico, and was at its height in the early 1500s. But in 1521 Aztec rule came to a sudden end. The Aztecs lost their empire to a small band of Spanish treasure-seekers.

Aztec warrior chiefs wore feather headdresses (feathers and jaguar skins were traded throughout the empire). But most people wore simple clothes woven from plant fibres.

THE AZTECS came to dominate other Native Americans in Central America by fighting constant wars with them. Their capital, Tenochtitlan, was founded in 1325 on an island in the middle of Lake Texcoco (now the site of Mexico City). Tenochtitlan was a walled city of 100,000 people, with stone temples and a network of canals. Causeways linked the main island to the mainland, and smaller islands were specially built as a place to grow vegetables.

Like the Maya, the Aztecs built pyramid-temples. This Mayan pyramid at Uxmal gives an idea of what the Aztec Great Temple at Tenochtitlan may have looked like before it was destroyed.

| c. 1200 | 1325 | 1440–1469 | 1500 | 1502 | 1519 |
|---------|------|-----------|------|------|------|
| Aztecs settle in the Valley of Mexico. | Traditional date for the founding of Tenochtitlan. | Reign of Montezuma I. The empire is extended. | The empire is at its height. The Aztecs rule more than 10 million people, most of whom belong to other tribes. | Montezuma II becomes emperor. | Spaniards led by Hernando Cortés march on Tenochtitlan. They are aided by tribes hostile to the Aztecs. |

The great Calendar Stone shows the face of the Sun-god Tonatiuh. The stone measures .7 m across and weighs about 25 tonnes. It was unearthed in Mexico City in 1790.

The Aztecs were skilled in sculpture, poetry, music and engineering. They worshipped the Sun as the giver of all life. Each year priests sacrificed thousands of victims to the Sun-god, cutting out their hearts as offerings, in the belief that this would bring good harvests and prosperity. Other sacrificial victims were drowned or beheaded.

Farmers grew corn, beans and tomatoes, and merchants traded throughout the empire. The ruling class were warriors. All warriors had to capture at least one enemy for sacrifice, and conquered peoples were forced to pay taxes to the emperor.

In 1519 Spanish treasure-seekers led by Hernando Cortés attacked the Aztecs. Emperor Montezuma II welcomed them, believing Cortés was the god Quetzalcoatl, but he was taken prisoner. Aztec spears and clubs were no match for Spanish guns, and by 1521 the Aztec empire was at an end.

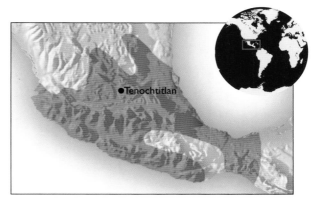

●Tenochtitlan

The heart of the Aztec empire was the fertile Valley of Mexico, where the capital, Tenochtitlan, and most of the major cities were located. These thrived as busy market centres. The empire extended east into present-day Guatemala.

## GODS AND SACRIFICE

One of the reasons that the Aztecs went to war was to capture prisoners, for sacrifice to the gods. They believed that the hearts and blood of their victims nourished the gods. Priests cut open the bodies using sacrificial knives like the one above. Sacrifices had to be performed on the right day, according to the sacred 260-day calendar.

| 20 | 1521 |
|---|---|
| The Aztecs rise up against the Spanish invaders. Montezuma wounded and dies. | Cortés and his men attack and capture Tenochtitlan. End of the Aztec empire. |

# The Incas

FROM the mountains of Peru, the god-emperor of the Incas ruled a highly organized empire. Civil war and Spanish invasion finally caused the empire to fall.

A mosaic mask made from mussel shells. Masks of gods' faces were worn by Inca priests for ceremonies, and were often richly decorated.

THE INCAS took over from the Chimu as rulers of the Andes mountains of South America. Their civilization reached its peak in the 1400s under the ruler Pachacuti, who defeated an invading army from a neighbouring state.

Pachacuti reformed the way the kingdom was run. He appointed a central administration to control the building of towns and ensure that farms and workshops were run efficiently. From the capital, Cuzco, he and his successors expanded the Inca empire to include parts of Chile, Bolivia and Ecuador.

The Incas communicated over long distances by sending fast runners with messages in the form of quipus (knotted cords). A message could be sent more than 200 km in a day along a system of paved roads.

The Incas built stone cities and fine roads, which were used by traders. Goods were bartered – exchanged for goods of equal value (the Incas did not use money). Farmers terraced the mountain slopes to grow corn, cotton and potatoes. Although they had neither writing nor wheeled vehicles, the Incas' many skills included music, bridge-building and medicine.

In 1525 the Inca empire was at its greatest extent. But in 1527, after Emperor Huayna Capac died, the empire was split between his two sons and civil war broke out. In the 1530s a Spanish expedition led by Francisco Pizarro arrived, seeking gold. The Europeans were impressed by Cuzco's

| 1200 | 1438 |
|---|---|
| Incas begin to conquer neighbouring peoples in the Andes region. | Inca empire starts, under Pachacuti, the 9th Inca (king). He fights off an invasion from a neighbouring state, the Chanca, and rebuilds Cuzco as the capital. |

palaces, temples and water supply, and by the fortress of Sacsahuaman, which was built from huge stones that fitted together perfectly without mortar.

A gold raft depicting El Dorado, a legendary ruler whose body was said to be dusted with gold every year. Such tales made European invaders greedy for gold.

Though few in number, the Spaniards had horses and guns, which were both new to the Incas. In 1532, Pizarro

The Spanish were fewer in number than the Incas. But they had horses, armour and guns. Many Incas fought bravely, but with their king murdered, they were quickly defeated.

captured the Inca ruler Atahualpa and demanded for a ransom a room full of gold and two rooms full of silver. The ransom was paid, but Atahualpa was killed anyway. The leaderless Inca armies were swiftly defeated, although resistance to Spanish rule continued from scattered mountain forts, such as Machu Picchu, until 1572.

**450–1500**
nder Topa Inca and his son, uayna Capac, the empire is xtended from Peru into odern-day Bolivia, Chile, cuador and Colombia.

**1525**
About this time, the first potatoes are taken to Europe from South America.

**1527**
Death of the emperor Huayna Capac; civil war starts between his sons Atahualpa and Huascar.

**1532**
Atahualpa defeats Huascar, who is imprisoned and later killed. Francisco Pizarro, with 167 soldiers, attacks Atahualpa's forces and captures Cuzco.

# Voyages of Discovery

IN THE late 1400s, Europeans began to explore the oceans. In stronger ships capable of longer voyages, they went in search of trade, treasure and new lands. Their voyages took them west to the Americas and east to Asia.

AFTER THE Byzantine empire fell to the Ottoman Turks in 1453, the old land trade routes between Europe and Asia were cut off. Europeans anxious to get spices – essential for flavouring and preserving their food – had to find a new way to reach India and the islands of Indonesia. This need, coupled with a growing curiosity and a spirit of adventure, sent Europeans to sea.

▶ European explorers sailed in ships called carracks with three masts and square sails. Columbus's ship "Santa Maria" probably looked like this.

First to go exploring were the Portuguese. Their prince, Henry the Navigator, took a keen interest in shipbuilding and navigation. He directed his sailors west into the Atlantic and south to explore the west coast of Africa. There they set up forts and traded for gold and ivory. Spanish, French, Dutch and English sailors followed. Some explorers, like Christopher Columbus, headed further west, and ended up in the Americas – much to their surprise.

Portugal and Spain began to settle and plunder the Americas, dividing it between them by treaty. By 1517 the Portuguese

◀ Seafarers used simple navigation instruments such as the astrolabe (top) and cross-staff to fix their ships' positions by sun and stars. The magnetic compass showed North, but was not always reliable

| 1419 | 1431 | 1488 | 1492 | 1494 | 1497 | 1500 |
|---|---|---|---|---|---|---|
| Portuguese sail to the Madeira Islands. | Portuguese reach the Azores. | Bartolomeu Dias of Portugal explores the west coast of Africa as far south as the Cape of Good Hope. | Christopher Columbus, an Italian, leads a Spanish expedition to America. | Spain and Portugal divide the Americas between them by the Treaty of Tordesillas. | John Cabot, an Italian in the service of England, sails to Canada. The Portuguese explorer Vasco Da Gama sails round Africa to India. | Pedro Alvares Cabral from Portugal sails to Brazil, South America. |

had landed in China (by sailing east around Africa to India and onward). Nearly 30 years later they reached Japan.

The ships used by the explorers were small, but more seaworthy than the clumsy vessels of the Middle Ages. They used a mixture of square and lateen (triangular) sails for easier steering and greater manoeuvrability. Sailors had only crude maps and simple instruments to guide them on voyages that lasted many months. In 1519 a Portuguese captain, Ferdinand Magellan, set out from Spain with five ships. The ships sailed around South America, across the Pacific Ocean to the Philippines (where Magellan was

## NEW WORLD FOODS

As well as gold and silver, European explorers brought back new foods from the Americas. Potatoes, tomatoes and peppers, plants native to America, were all unknown in Europe before 1500. Potatoes were at first a luxury, served only to the rich at banquets. Chocolate, from the cacao tree, was first brought to Spain from Mexico in 1520. Also from the New World came tobacco, turkeys and maize.

killed) and across the Indian Ocean to Africa. Only one ship, commanded by Sebastian Del Cano, found its way home to Spain, becoming the first ship to sail around the world.

▶ The voyages of discovery revealed to Europeans that the world was larger than ancient geographers had believed. Sailors crossed oceans and met peoples unknown to earlier Europeans.

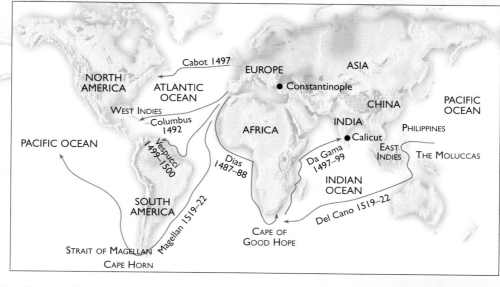

1501
Italian Amerigo Vespucci sails to South America. A map published in 1507 names the continent "America" after him.

1509
Spain begins settlement of the Americas.

1513
Spanish explorer Vasco Nuñez de Balboa is the first European to see the Pacific.

1517
Portuguese traders reach China.

1522
First round-the-world voyage is completed by Ferdinand Magellan's Spanish crew.

1524
Italian Giovanni da Verrazano searches for a northwest passage from Europe to Asia.

# Spain and Portugal

**M**EDIEVAL Spain was divided between Christian and Muslim kingdoms. After wars, two Christian monarchs ended Muslim rule in Spain: they were Ferdinand of Aragon and Isabella of Castile.

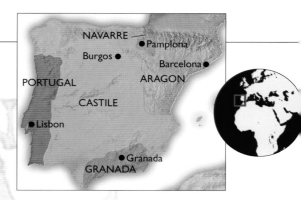

In the early 1400s, Spain was not yet one kingdom. Aragon and Castile were the strongest Christian kingdoms, while Granada was ruled by Muslim emirs.

IN 1469 Ferdinand and Isabella were married, uniting Spain's two strongest Christian kingdoms. By 1492 their forces had captured Granada, the last Muslim outpost in Spain. The new rulers were intolerant of other religions and set up the Spanish Inquisition to seek out heretics – both Christians who held different beliefs from the Roman Catholic Church and people of other faiths, such as Jews.

In the 16th century, Spain became Europe's strongest nation. Its army fought wars in Europe (against the Dutch, for example) and its navy controlled the profitable trade in gold and silver from Spain's new empire in the Americas.

Catherine of Aragon (1485–1536) was the daughter of King Ferdinand and Queen Isabella of Spain. In 1509 she became the first of the six wives of King Henry VIII of England.

Columbus leaves the court of Spain, having won the support of King Ferdinand and Queen Isabella for his westward voyage. He set sail in 1492, convinced that the Atlantic was a narrow ocean.

| 711 | Early 1000s | 1143 | Late 1200s | 1479 | 1492 | 1512 |
|---|---|---|---|---|---|---|
| Muslims invade southern Spain (which includes what later becomes Portugal). | Muslim central rule of Spain collapses in civil war. | Portugal gains independence from Castile. | Granada is the only Moorish kingdom in Spain. | Aragon and Castile become one kingdom. | Moors are forced out of Granada. Jews are expelled from Spain. Columbus sails to America. | Ferdinand seize Navarre to complete unification of Spain. |

Spanish power reached its peak during the reign of Charles I (1516–1556). He became Holy Roman emperor in 1519, which gave him control of lands in Germany, Austria and the Netherlands, as well as parts of France and Italy. On his death, his lands were divided between his son Philip II (who ruled Spain, the Netherlands and Spanish colonies in the Americas) and his brother Ferdinand (who became Holy Roman emperor).

By 1580, the Spanish empire included Portugal. Portugal had led the way in European exploration of the oceans. Its sailors had opened up new trade routes to Asia. The Portuguese already controlled an overseas empire that included large stretches of coastline in East and West Africa, Brazil and India, as well as trading posts such as Goa in India, Macao in China and many islands in Southeast Asia.

◁ Arabic script on Spanish stonework. The Muslims left a rich legacy of architecture in cities such as Granada and Cordoba in southern Spain.

▷ Philip II ruled Spain from 1556 to 1598. A devout Catholic, he dreamed of a Spanish-led Catholic empire embracing Europe and America.

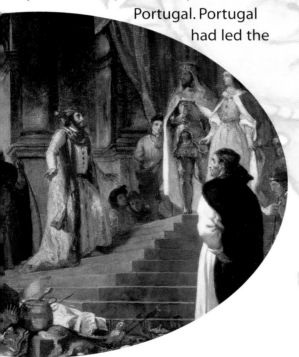

## HENRY THE NAVIGATOR

Prince Henry of Portugal (1394–1460) had a passion to explore. He brought together seamen, shipbuilders and mapmakers to plan voyages in carracks and caravels (right).

| 1521 | 1535 | 1556 | 1565 | 1568 | 1571 | 1580 | 1588 |
|---|---|---|---|---|---|---|---|
| Spain conquers the Aztec empire in Mexico. | Spain conquers the Inca empire in Peru. | Philip II becomes king of Spain. The Spanish empire is at its height. | Spain colonizes the Philippines. | War in the Spanish Netherlands begins. | Battle of Lepanto: Spain and Austria defeat a Turkish fleet. | Spain conquers Portugal and holds it until 1640. | Spanish Armada sails to invade England, but fails. |

# African Empires

AFRICA was a continent of many kingdoms and empires. The richest African rulers commanded trade in gold, ivory and slaves – goods that by 1500 were attracting European traders.

KANEM BORNU

Timbuktu ● ● Gao ● Ngazergama

SONGHAI

Axum ●

ETHIOPIA

KONGO

GREAT ZIMBABWE

◢ African kingdoms, c. 1400–1600. Because transport across much of Africa was so difficult, Africans often had more contact with Europeans and Asians (who traded with them by sea) than with other African states.

◢ Timbuktu, on the southern edge of the Sahara Desert, was the centre of the gold and salt trade, and merchants came from as far as Morocco to sell cloth and horses there. Muslim scholars from the city advised the ruler of the Songhai empire, Askia Muhammad I.

PORTUGUESE traders sailing the coast of West Africa heard tales of wondrous kingdoms in the heart of the continent. The strongest was Songhai, a Muslim kingdom that controlled trade across the Sahara Desert. In 1464 King Sonni Ali freed Songhai from control by the Mali empire, and expanded its borders. A new Songhai dynasty was founded in 1493 by Askia Muhammad I, who gained great wealth from the trading cities of Jenne and Timbuktu. Songhai rule lasted until 1591, when the army was defeated by a Moroccan force, which was better-armed with guns.

| 1300s | 1335 | 1341 | 1430s | 1460s | 1464 | 1468 | From 1480s |
|---|---|---|---|---|---|---|---|
| European rulers try to contact the legendary Prester John. Great Zimbabwe is the heart of a powerful Bantu kingdom. | The Songhai ruling dynasty is founded. | Suleiman is king of Mali to 1360. | Portuguese begin exploring the west coast of Africa. | Portuguese explorers buy ivory, pepper, palm oil and slaves from the kingdom of Benin. | Songhai breaks away from Mali's control. | Sonni Ali captures Timbuktu. | Portuguese traders set up forts as bases to trade with African rulers. |

Another Muslim empire, Kanem-Bornu, extended through parts of present-day Chad, Cameroon, Nigeria, Niger and Libya. Kanem-Bornu thrived on trade between northern and southern Africa. It reached its peak about 1570, under Idris Alawma.

In northeast Africa was the Christian empire of Ethiopia. Europeans heard tales of its legendary ruler, Prester John. Here, people lived by farming and cattle-herding.

◀ Great Zimbabwe as it looks today, with parts of its massive defensive walls still standing. In the 1400s the walled citadel was surrounded by village houses and grazing cattle.

By 1450 a settlement at Great Zimbabwe in southern Africa was at its greatest extent. Built over about 400 years, Great Zimbabwe was probably a royal stronghold. It was surrounded by massive walls and a high tower. The people of this prosperous kingdom used copper and iron, and traded in gold with Sofala on the east coast (present-day Mozambique). By 1500, however, the civilization that built it was in decline.

◀ Ethiopian Christians cut down into solid rock to build their cross-shaped churches, which were hollowed out inside. Fifteen rock churches survive at Lalibela (then named Roha), capital of the Ethiopian empire in the 1200s.

### PRESTER JOHN

Travellers told tales of Prester ("priest") John, the fabulously rich Christian king of Ethiopia. One story claimed he had a magic mirror in which he could see everything that went on in his empire. Another story tells of giant ants that dug up gold for his treasury.

| 1488 | 1493 | 1506 | 1511 | 1520 | c. 1530 | 1591 |
|---|---|---|---|---|---|---|
| Portuguese explorer Bartolomeu Dias rounds the Cape of Good Hope. | Songhai is at its peak. Askia Muhammad I takes over the Mandingo empire. | The kingdom of Kongo has its first Christian king, Afonso I. | A Portuguese explorer reaches Great Zimbabwe, now in decline. | Portuguese mission to Ethiopia (lasts until 1526). | The slave trade from Africa to the Americas begins. | Songhai is defeated by Moroccans, aided by Spanish and Portuguese soldiers. |

# The Reformation

THE REFORMATION was a protest movement to reform the Catholic Church. It came about at a time when there was a new interest in humanism – the belief that humans are in control of their own destinies. Aware of the growing discontent with the way the Western Christian Church was run, reformers suggested new forms of worship, to create a new relationship between the people, Church and God.

◄ Martin Luther believed that people were saved by faith alone, that the Bible was central to that faith, and that church services should be in everyday languages, not in Latin.

IN 1517 Martin Luther, a German monk, protested publicly at what he saw as the Church's corruption and called for reform. His campaign led to a religious movement known as the Reformation. His ideas were taken up and spread by other reformers, such as Ulrich Zwingli in Switzerland and John Calvin in France. This led to the formation of Protestant ("protesting") Churches.

The technology of printing spread these ideas. The Bible, which previously had been available only in Latin (the language of scholars) was translated into local languages for all to read. Some rulers used discontent

▶ King Henry VIII made himself head of the Church in England. He always considered himself a Catholic, despite his quarrel with the Pope in Rome over his divorce from Catherine of Aragon.

**1498**
Savonarola, an Italian friar who preached Church reform, is burned at the stake in Florence.

**1517**
Martin Luther pins 95 written arguments critical of the Catholic Church on a church door in Wittenberg, Germany. This sets off the Reformation.

**1519**
Ulrich Zwingli starts the Reformation in Switzerland.

**1521**
Luther is expelled from the Church.

**1532**
John Calvin starts the Protestant movement in France.

**1534**
Ignatius Loyola founds the Jesuits. Henry VIII becomes head of the Church of England.

**1536**
Dissolution of the monasteries in England.

ith the Church for their own ends. enry VIII of England, for example, anted to divorce Catherine of Aragon. 'hen the Pope refused to grant the ivorce, Henry broke with the Church in ome to get his own way.

From 1545 the Catholic Church fought ack with a movement known as the ounter Reformation. It sent out Jesuit riests to campaign against the spread f Protestantism and convert the eoples of the Spanish empire. The split etween Christians in Western Europe d to wars as countries struggled with ew religious alliances. Catholics and rotestants persecuted one another, ften in the cruellest ways.

John Calvin, religious reformer, was born in France. He believed that only people chosen by God would be saved from damnation. His reforms became known as "Calvinism".

The Spanish sent the Armada against England in 1588 to restore Catholic rule. An English fireship attack off Calais helped fight off the planned invasion. The great Spanish fleet was eventually wrecked by storms around the coasts of northern Britain.

| 541 | 1549 | 1562 | 1568 | 1581 | 1588 | 1598 |
|---|---|---|---|---|---|---|
| hn Knox kes the eformation Scotland. | A new prayer book, the *Book of Common Prayer*, is introduced in England. | Religious wars in France between Catholics and Huguenots (Protestants). | Protestant Dutch revolt against Spanish rule. | The Netherlands declares independence from Spain (not recognized by Spain until 1648). | Defeat of the Spanish Armada off Britain's coasts. | Edict of Nantes gives Protestants and Catholics in France equal rights. |

# The Thirty Years' War

THE RELIGIOUS conflicts in Europe that started after the Reformation continued into the 1600s. The Thirty Years' War began in 1618 as a protest by the Protestant noblemen of Bohemia (now part of the Czech Republic) against their Catholic rulers, the Holy Roman emperors.

BOHEMIA'S noblemen chose Protestant Frederick of Bohemia to become their king. Then, in 1619, Ferdinand II, a member of the powerful Habsburg royal family, became the new Holy Roman emperor. Determined to turn the empire back to Catholicism, Ferdinand sent his army to attack Bohemia.

By 1620 Ferdinand's army had forced Frederick and his family to flee to the Netherlands. Catholicism was now the only form of Christianity allowed in Bohemia. A year later Spain, also ruled by the Habsburgs, joined the war on the side of the Holy Roman empire and sent an army to fight the Protestant Dutch. In 1625 the Dutch asked Denmark and England for help. Many English soldiers died not by fighting, but from plague, and by 1629 Habsburg armies had also defeated the Danes.

The Protestant Swedish king Gustavus II Adolphus led his army to war against

⬆ In 1618, a group of Bohemian nobles threw two Catholic governors out of a window in Prague Castle. This act, known now as the Defenestration of Prague, sparked off the Thirty Years' War.

▶ King Gustavus II Adolphus of Sweden leading his troops into battle, as was his custom. He went to war against the Habsburgs to defend Protestant beliefs, and also to protect Swedish trade in the Baltic, which was being threatened by Spain.

| 1618 | 1619 | 1620 | 1625–1629 | 1630 | 1631 |
|---|---|---|---|---|---|
| War starts with the Defenestration of Prague. | Ferdinand II is crowned Holy Roman emperor. | Ferdinand's army enters Bohemia and defeats Protestant King Frederick. | Denmark and England join the war in support of the Dutch. | King Gustavus II Adolphus of Sweden joins the war on the side of the Protestants. | Swedish victory at the battle of Breitenfeld. |

## PURITANS

Puritans were Protestants who wanted to "purify" the Church of England of its bishops and ritual. They dressed in simple clothes. The Pilgrim Fathers were Puritans.

▶ Oliver Cromwell (1599–1658). He helped recruit, train and command the New Model Army, his "Ironsides". As Lord Protector he tried to impose parliamentary rule in Scotland and Ireland by force.

...upport and Charles ...eft London. Both sides then raised ...rmies of volunteers.

Neither side won the first major battle, ...ought in August 1642 at Edgehill. ...hanks largely to Cromwell's New Model ...rmy, Parliament beat the Royalists at ...Marston Moor (1644) and, decisively, at ...aseby (1645). Charles fled to the Scots, ...who handed him over to Parliament. He ...scaped and plotted with ...he Scots to fight again ...1648), but his forces ...vere soon crushed. ...le was tried for ...reason, found ...uilty, and

executed in January 1649. In 1651 his son Charles, invading with Scots help, was beaten at Worcester. This battle ended the Civil War. England was governed as a Commonwealth (republic) by Parliament, until its members quarrelled. From 1653, Oliver Cromwell ruled as Lord Protector, backed by his army. When he died in 1658, his son Richard was soon removed from office. In 1660 a new Parliament invited Charles II back from exile.

▶ The execution ...f King Charles I ...ok place in ...Vhitehall on 31 ...anuary 1649.

| ...46 | 1647 | 1648 | 1649 | 1651 | 1653–1658 | 1660 |
|---|---|---|---|---|---|---|
| ...harles ...rrenders to ...e Scots. | Charles is handed over to Parliament. He escapes to the Isle of Wight. | Charles, aided by Scots, starts second civil war, but is defeated. | Charles goes on trial for treason. He is executed on 31 January. | Charles's son goes into exile in France. | Cromwell rules as Lord Protector. | Restoration of the monarchy; Charles II comes to the throne. |

# Revolution and Industry

## THE WORLD IN TURMOIL 1700–1900

**T**HE TWO centuries between 1700 and 1900 were a time of conflict, revolution and change in many parts of the world. Empires were won and lost, kings and governments toppled, and agriculture, industry and transport developed rapidly.

THE COUNTRIES of northwest Europe grew more powerful, while Spain and Portugal declined. The 13 American colonies declared their independence from Britain in 1776 to become the United States of America. They were helped by the French who in 1789 had their own revolution. The French overthrew their king and became first a republic and then an empire. By 1793 this action had led to wars between France and Austria, Britain, the Netherlands, Portugal, Prussia, Russia and Spain. The wars lasted until 1815 when the French emperor Napoleon was finally defeated.

**1644**
Manchus overthrow the Ming dynasty of China.

**1682–1725**
Peter the Great rules Russia.

**1740**
Frederick the Great becomes king of Prussia, which dominates Europe.

**1756–1763**
Seven Years' War: France, Austria and Russia clash with Britain and Prussia.

**1768**
James Cook's first of three voyages to the Pacific.

**1769**
James Watt builds the first efficient steam engine.

**1776, 4 July**
The Continental Congress in America adopts the Declaration of Independence.

**1789, 14 July**
A mob seizes the Bastille in Paris. Start of the French Revolution.

The Spanish and Portuguese colonies in South America took advantage of the wars in Europe to gain their independence, and by 1830 were all free of foreign rule. Later conflicts in Europe united the separate states of Germany and of Italy into two countries. In the United States of America, conflict over slavery led to a four-year civil war.

Revolutions in agriculture, industry and transport affected the lives of even more people, especially in Europe and America. Canals and railways made travel overland easier, while steam-powered ships were faster than sailing ships had been. New methods of farming made it possible to feed more people, and large numbers left the countryside to make a living in the rapidly expanding towns. Factories in towns used machines to produce vast quantities of goods once made by hand.

To provide raw materials and a ready market for these factory goods, many European countries built up empires overseas. Britain tightened its control on India and laid claim to Australia and New Zealand. In the Scramble for Africa (1880 to 1900), European powers divided most of Africa between them. China, Japan and Russia stayed largely isolated from the rest of the world. The rising power was the United States, where millions of Europeans settled, their westward movement forcing Native Americans from their ancient homelands.

| 91 | 1804 | 1808 | 1830 | 1837–1901 | 1848 | 1857 | 1861–1865 | 1869 |
|---|---|---|---|---|---|---|---|---|
| omas ine's *The ghts of an* is blished. | Napoleon declares himself emperor of France. | Independence struggles begin in South America. | First all-steam railway, in England. | Queen Victoria's reign; the British empire includes a quarter of the world's people. | Year of Revolutions affects most of Europe. | Indian Mutiny. | The American Civil War. | Union Pacific Railroad links east and west coasts of America. |

# The Russian Empire

PETER THE GREAT changed Russia from an isolated, backward nation into a major European power. Nearly 40 years after his death, another great ruler, Catherine the Great, carried on his ambition.

⬆ The Summer Palace and St Petersburg's other grand buildings and palaces were built by European architects for Peter the Great. The city was built on many islands, linked by bridges

1639, but it was still backward compared with the rest of Europe. Peter was determined to change this. For 18 months he toured Europe, meeting king scientists and people in industry, farmin and ship-building. In the Netherlands he even worked in a shipyard for a while. When he returned to Russia, Peter put th knowledge he had gained to use. He bu

IN 1682, aged just 10, Peter the Great (Peter I) became tsar of Russia. At first he ruled with his half-brother Ivan V. When Ivan died in 1696, Peter ruled on his own until 1725. Russia had been expanding rapidly since

⬇ Throughout the long Russian winters, carriages used runners instead of wheels, so th could glide through th snow like a sleigh.

⬆ Peter the Great ruled Russia from 1682 to 1725. He was an immensely tall, strong, energetic man. But he could also be brutal – he imprisoned and tortured his own son, for example.

| 1672 | 1696 | 1700–1721 | 1703 | 1712 | 1722–1723 | 1725 | 1729 |
|------|------|-----------|------|------|-----------|------|------|
| Peter the Great is born. | Peter becomes sole ruler of Russia. | Great Northern War against Sweden. | St Petersburg is founded. Peter calls it his "window on Europe". | St Petersburg becomes Russia's capital and main port. | War with Persia gives Russia access to the Caspian Sea. | Peter the Great dies. | The future Catherine the Great is born in Prussia. |

up the navy and encouraged industries and farming. He improved and expanded the army and built new roads and canals to help trade.

Peter also gained a Baltic coastline for Russia through war with Sweden. This gave Russia a seaport that was not ice-bound in winter. He moved Russia's capital from Moscow to St Petersburg on the Baltic. Under Peter, the serfs (peasants) were made to pay more tax, and were worse off. But in 1725, when Peter died, Russia as a whole was more secure and advanced than it had been when he came to power.

In 1762, another powerful ruler came to the throne. Catherine II (the Great) was Prussian by birth, but married the heir to the Russian throne in 1745. He was murdered six months after he

◀ Catherine the Great was ruthless and ambitious. She was interested in new ideas, but her plans to improve Russia's education system and reform the law came to nothing.

became tsar, and Catherine declared herself empress. Like Peter, she encouraged western ideas and gained territory for Russia, fighting the Ottoman empire in 1774 and 1792, and Sweden in 1790. She also claimed much of Poland. Conditions did not improve for the serfs, however, and a revolt in 1773 was harshly put down.

▶ Life was a constant struggle for Russia's serfs. They paid heavy taxes and, if the harvest was bad, often went hungry.

| 1745 | 1762 | 1773 | 1787 | 1796 |
|------|------|------|------|------|
| Catherine marries her cousin, Peter I, heir to the Russian throne. | Catherine becomes empress of Russia after her husband's death. | A revolt by the serfs is brutally crushed. | On a tour of Russia, Catherine meets healthy, well-fed, well-dressed actors while the real serfs are hidden from sight. | Catherine dies and is succeeded by her son. |

# The Enlightenment

THE ENLIGHTENMENT was the name given to a time of new ideas, beginning in the 1600s and lasting until the end of the 1700s. It was also called the Age of Reason, because people began to look for reasons why things happened as they did. Modern science grew out of this questioning. New ideas about government and how people should live were also central to the Enlightenment.

▶ The *Encyclopédie*, compiled by the French writer and critic Denis Diderot, was written by experts in many subjects and aimed to cover all branches of knowledge. First published between 1751 and 1772, the work comprised 17 volumes text and 11 volumes of pictures.

SOME EUROPEAN RULERS took up Enlightenment ideas with enthusiasm. S did ordinary people who were no longe willing to be told what to do, and wante a say in government. Others feared that the new thinking would overturn the ol world for ever. The French philosopher René Descartes (1596–1650) argued that only an idea that could be

▶ The telescope opened new worlds of discovery. Improved telescopes made by Newton in 1668 and Cassegrain in 1672 used mirrors to reflect light, and gave astronomers clearer images of the Universe.

▶ A botanical drawing of sunflowers from *Philosophia Botanica* by Carl von Linné (Linnaeus), published in 1751. Linnaeus was the first person to classify the plant and animal kingdoms, defining and grouping living things into species.

**1632–1704**
Life of English philosopher John Locke. He believed that all men were equal and free and that the authority of government comes only from the consent of the governed.

**1687**
Sir Isaac Newton sets out his theories about light and the visible spectrum, the three laws of motion and the existence of gravity.

**1743**
Benjamin Franklin sets up the American Philosophical Society in Philadelphia. Its members are interested in science as well as philosophy.

**1743–1794**
Life of French chemist Antoine Lavoisier, who was first to establish that combustion (burning) is a form of chemical action.

## INFLUENTIAL WOMEN

New ideas were exchanged at meetings of artistic and educated people. They gathered, often in the homes of wealthy women, to discuss the latest scientific discoveries, plays, books and issues of the day. Two such women were Madame Geoffrin, seen here in 1725, and Marie-Anne Lavoisier, wife of the chemist Antoine Lavoisier.

inventor and statesman, Adam Smith the economist, David Hume the historian, the philosopher Immanuel Kant and the writer Mary Wollstonecraft. The belief that every person had the right to knowledge, freedom and happiness inspired a new revolutionary and democratic fervour, which was to shape the world of the 19th century.

hown to be true, by evidence or by easoning, was true. Such arguments roubled the Christian Church, and also kings and queens who believed they had a "divine" (God-given) right to ule. Another French thinker, Voltaire (1694–1778), criticized both the Church and government of his day. So did Jean-Jacques Rousseau (1712–1778), whose ideas helped shape the events leading to the American and French revolutions. Other leading lights of the Enlightenment were Benjamin Franklin, scientist,

> François Marie Arouet used the pen-name Voltaire. He was a scientist, thinker and writer, noted for his wit. He declared: "I may disagree with what you say, but I will defend to the death your right to say it."

# Austria and Prussia

EUROPE in the 18th century was dominated by absolute monarchs. Rulers of all they surveyed, they built magnificent palaces and attracted artists, musicians and intellectuals to their "enlightened" courts. Two of the richest and most powerful states were Austria and Prussia.

The Schonbrunn Palace in Vienna (built 1696–1711) was the Habsburgs' summer palace. Planned to rival Versailles, it had 1,440 rooms.

AUSTRIA was ruled by the Habsburgs, a family that had dominated Europe since the 13th century. In the early 1500s Charles V, then Holy Roman Emperor, divided his huge realm. One half was ruled from Spain, the other from Vienna in Austria. In 1700 the Spanish Habsburgs died out, but the Austrian

Maria Theresa (1717–1780) inherited the throne of Austria in 1740. War broke out among her rivals, but her position was secured in 1748.

Wolfgang Amadeus Mozart (1756–1791) playing at the court of Maria Theresa. Mozart first played at court when he was only six years old.

| 1700 | 1711 | 1713 | 1740 | 1756–1763 |
|---|---|---|---|---|
| Austria has taken Hungary from the Ottomans. The last Spanish Habsburg monarch dies and Spain is ruled by the Bourbons of France. | Charles VI, Archduke of Austria, becomes Holy Roman Emperor. | Frederick William succeeds as king of Prussia. | Maria Theresa succeeds Charles VI. Rivals challenge her right to rule. Frederick II (the Great) becomes king of Prussia. | Seven Years' War. France, Austria and Russia clash with Britain and Prussia. |

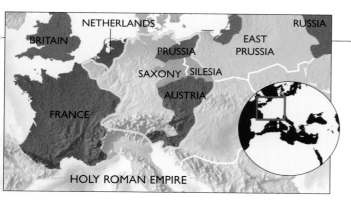

HOLY ROMAN EMPIRE

◄ In the Seven Years' War (1756–1763), France, Austria and Russia opposed Prussia and Britain. At the end of the war Prussia gained Silesia, seized from Austria. Britain took control of France's colonies in India and America.

Habsburgs were still powerful. From 1740 a woman, Maria Theresa, ruled Austria (which included Hungary, recaptured from the Turks). She restored its power and made Vienna the artistic centre of Europe. Artists from all over Europe came to work on its grand building projects. Maria Theresa was succeeded in 1780 by her son Joseph II, a follower of the Enlightenment, though no democrat, who freed the serfs and abolished privileges enjoyed by nobles.

Frederick II (the Great) became king of Prussia in 1740. An outstanding general, he inherited a well-organized state with a powerful army, which he used to make Prussia a major power.

► Frederick the Great (1712–1786) of Prussia was a cultured man, but also a stern administrator. He encouraged the study of science and agriculture, and improved education.

# Birth of the United States

**B**Y THE MID-1700s there were 13 British colonies in North America. Britain had also won control of Canada, by defeating France in the Seven Years' War (1756–1763). Britain had no thought of changing the way it governed its American colonies, but the colonists, denied a say in governing themselves, rebelled. The American Revolution led to the colonies' independence as the United States.

The Declaration of Independence was signed on 4 July 1776, by delegates from the 13 colonies. It separated them from Great Britain and created the United States.

BRITAIN taxed its American citizens to help pay for the defence of North America. There were about two million British-Americans. They produced most of their own food and other goods, but were unhappy at having to pay taxes on imported tea and legal documents. The Americans had no representatives in the British Parliament, and declared that "taxation without representation is

British troops, trained for fighting in European wars, found fighting in America very different. Standing in close-packed ranks, firing volleys of shot, they presented good targets for the American sharpshooters. British infantrymen (left) wore red long-tailed coats, and so were known as "redcoats".

On Christmas night, 1776, George Washington led his troops across the icy Delaware River and went on to defeat the British at the battle of Trenton. This was one of the first major American victories in the War of Independence.

| **1765** | **1770** | **1773** | **1775** | **1776** | **1777** |
|---|---|---|---|---|---|
| Protests start against British taxes in the American colonies. | At the Boston Massacre, British troops fire on a crowd of colonists and kill five of them. | The Boston Tea Party; in Boston harbour, colonists throw ships' cargoes overboard as a protest against the tax on tea. | The American War of Independence starts. | On 4 July, the Continental Congress adopts the Declaration of Independence. | The British are defeated at Saratoga, New York. France sides with America. The British capture Philadelphia, Pennsylvania. |

yranny". Britain reacted by sending soldiers. In April 1775, an armed confrontation between colonists and British troops took place at Lexington in Massachusetts. The colonists formed an army of their own, commanded by George Washington, and on 17 June the two armies clashed at Bunker Hill, near Boston. The British were successful, but the War of Independence, or American Revolution, had begun.

While fighting continued, colonial leaders signed the

## PAUL REVERE

Paul Revere is one of the heroes of the War of Independence. He rode from Boston to Lexington to warn of the approach of British soldiers. Although he was captured, his mission was successful. Revere was immortalized in a famous poem by Longfellow.

Declaration of Independence on 4 July 1776. The British government refused to accept it. Under Washington's command, the colonists' army began to defeat the British. France, Spain and the Netherlands all joined the colonists' side. The six-year war ended in 1781, when the British surrendered at Yorktown. Two years later, Britain recognized the independent United States of America.

| 1778 | 1779 | 1780 | 1781 |
|------|------|------|------|
| The British capture Savannah, Georgia. | Spain joins the war on America's side. | The Dutch join the war on America's side. British victory at Charleston, South Carolina. | After a siege at Yorktown, Virginia, the British surrender. |

# The French Revolution

THE FRENCH Revolution of 1789 shook all of Europe. It began as a protest for fairness, food and democracy. The French people, most of whom were denied a say in government, rose up against the "old order". The years of bloodshed led to the emergence of a dictator, who made himself emperor – Napoleon Bonaparte.

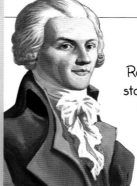

In 1793, Maximilien Robespierre (1758–1794) started the Reign of Terror. Over the next nine months thousands of opponents of the Revolution were put to death, until he himself was denounced and guillotined.

IN THE 18TH CENTURY, society in France was divided into three classes, or estates. The first estate was the nobility, the second was the clergy and the third was everyone else. Only people in the third estate paid taxes. Educated people, by now familiar with the ideas of the Enlightenment, knew how unfair the system was. Their discontent increased in 1788, when a bad harvest pushed up prices, leaving many people facing starvation. After years of extravagant kings and costly wars, the government had little money to deal with the crisis. When, in 1789, King Louis XVI called a meeting of the Estates General (the nearest France had to a parliament) to raise more money, the third estate said that if they had to pay taxes, they should have a say in how the country was run. Louis XVI refused this request.

The rebels, calling themselves the National Assembly, refused to leave Versailles until the king listened to their demands.

During the Reign of Terror about 500,000 people were arrested and 17,000 of them put to death by public execution on the guillotine. Many of the first victims were aristocrats, condemned as "enemies of the people".

| 1789, 15 May | 1789, 14 July | 1789, 26 August | 1789, 5 October | 1791 |
|---|---|---|---|---|
| The Estates General meets for the first time since 1614. The third estate breaks away and forms the National Assembly. | The French Revolution starts when a mob seizes the Bastille. | The Declaration of the Rights of Man is made. | The king and his family are seized by a mob and taken to Paris as prisoners. | The royal family try to escape but are returned to Paris. |

## MARIE ANTOINETTE

Marie Antoinette (1755–1793), daughter of Maria Theresa of Austria, was married to King Louis XVI of France. At first she was popular, but her extravagance soon turned people against her. On hearing that Parisians were rioting over bread shortages, she is reputed to have said: "Let them eat cake!"

n Paris a mob attacked the Bastille, a royal prison, and riots broke out all over France. The National Assembly made a Declaration of the Rights of Man. These included liberty, equality and the right to resist oppression. Louis XVI and his family were arrested and held until 1793. Finally, the king was put on trial and executed. This was the start of the Reign of Terror, led by Maximilien Robespierre, in which thousands of people were put to death. Austria, Britain, the Netherlands, Prussia and Spain all went to war with France. Alarmed by this turn of events, Robespierre's colleagues ordered his execution. The threat of civil war in 1795 led to the rise of an ambitious French soldier, Napoleon Bonaparte.

**1792**
nce is clared a ublic.

**1793**
Louis XVI is executed in January, Marie Antoinette in October. The Reign of Terror starts. The Netherlands, Austria, Britain, Prussia and Spain are at war with France.

**1794**
Robespierre's execution ends the Reign of Terror. France is governed by the Directoire, a committee of five.

**1795**
Napoleon Bonaparte's rise to power starts when he defends Paris against rebels.

# Australia and New Zealand

IN THE late 1700s, Europeans rediscovered Australia and New Zealand and the peoples living there, the Aboriginals and Maoris. Settlement of Australia by Britain began in 1788, and in 1840 New Zealand became a British colony. Emigrants from Europe settled in both countries.

A reconstruction of "Endeavour", the ship in which James Cook set out to explore the South Pacific in 1768. Scientists and artists on board recorded the plants, animals and people they saw or met on the voyage.

This map shows the voyages to Australia and New Zealand of the 17th-century Dutch explorers Willem Jansz and Abel Tasman, and the three epic explorations (1768–1779) of England's James Cook.

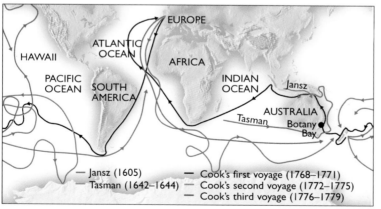

EUROPE
ATLANTIC OCEAN
HAWAII
AFRICA
PACIFIC OCEAN
SOUTH AMERICA
INDIAN OCEAN
Jansz
AUSTRALIA
Tasman
Botany Bay

— Jansz (1605)
— Tasman (1642–1644)
— Cook's first voyage (1768–1771)
— Cook's second voyage (1772–1775)
— Cook's third voyage (1776–1779)

BRITISH NAVIGATOR James Cook made three voyages to the Pacific during the 1700s. His first expedition left in 1768. Cook sailed around New Zealand, then to the eastern and northern coasts of Australia. He landed at Botany Bay on the southeast coast and claimed the territory for Britain. On his second journey he explored many of the Pacific islands. The third voyage, in 1776, took him back to New Zealand. He then explored the Pacific coast of South America, before sailing to Hawaii.

In 1788 the First Fleet sailed from Britain, transporting convicts to the penal colony of Port Jackson in Australia. Some prisoners stayed on as free men

| 1768–1771 | 1772–1775 | 1776 | 1788 | 1793 | 1803 | 1813 |
|---|---|---|---|---|---|---|
| Captain James Cook's first voyage to the South Pacific. | Captain Cook's second voyage to the South Pacific. | Captain Cook's third and last voyage to the South Pacific. In 1779 he is killed in a quarrel with Hawaiians. | Convicts are transported from Britain to Australia. | The first free settlers from Britain arrive in Australia. They settle in Botany Bay. | Settlers from Britain start going to Tasmania for the first time. | By this date merino sheep (from Spain) have been introduced into Australia. Settlers have spread north and west, beyond the Blue Mountains. |

## ABORIGINALS AND MAORIS

Many Aboriginal Australians were ill-treated by Europeans. Some were shot, others died from European diseases. Many simply lost the will to live. The Maoris of New Zealand numbered about 100,000 when James Cook arrived. After the Treaty of Waitangi, Maori rights were not protected, war broke out, and in 1848 the Maoris were defeated.

...nd from 1793 were joined by settlers, who made their homes around Botany ...ay. Towns were built and explorers crossed the continent. The settlers showed little respect for the Aboriginal

Australians whose lands they were taking. Transportation of convicts to Australia ended in 1850.

In New Zealand, the French arrived after Cook, but found the Maoris hostile. Contacts resumed with visits by whalers, seal-hunters and Christian missionaries in the early 1800s. In 1840, by the Treaty of Waitangi, Maori leaders gave up their lands and New Zealand became a British colony.

Captain James Cook and his men meet Maoris for the first time, while charting the coast of New Zealand (1769-1770). Cook was killed by islanders in Hawaii in 1779.

...40
...aori leaders sign the ...reaty of Waitangi. It offers ...nd rights and full British ...tizenship. The treaty is not ...onoured and war breaks ...ut (1843–1848).

1851
Discovery of gold in Victoria results in the Gold Rush.

# Napoleon's Wars

NAPOLEON Bonaparte (1769–1821) rose from the rank of artillery officer to become emperor of France. Determined to unify Europe under his rule, his wars of conquest dominated the start of the 19th century.

◁ In land battles, Napoleon was a master at using artillery (wheeled guns). At sea, he tried to starve Britain into making peace by cutting its trade links, but he was unable to defeat the British navy.

headed for Egypt, hoping to disrupt the British trade route to India. He defeated the Egyptians in 1798 at the battle of the Pyramids, but was then stranded when the British navy destroyed the French

NAPOLEON was born on the island of Corsica. He joined the French army in 1785. He supported the French Revolution and in 1793 defeated anti-revolutionary forces at Toulon. In 1795 he was called to Paris to defend the city against rebels, and in 1796 was appointed to command the French army in Italy. He won control of Italy from Austrian forces, and then

▷ At the battle of Austerlitz in December 1805, a French army of 73,000, under the command of Napoleon and his generals Soult and Bernadotte, defeated an army of 87,000 Austrians and Russians.

| 1785 | 1795 | 1797 | 1798 | 1799 | 1804 | 1805 |
|---|---|---|---|---|---|---|
| Napoleon becomes an officer in the French army. | Napoleon defends Paris against rebels and prevents civil war breaking out. | A French army led by Napoleon drives Austrians from much of northern Italy. | The French fleet is defeated by Nelson at the battle of the Nile in Egypt. | Napoleon returns to France and seizes power. | Napoleon declares himself emperor of France. | The French fleet is defeated by Nelson at the battle of Trafalgar. Napoleon's army defeats the Austrians and Russians at the battle of Austerlitz. |

eet at Aboukir Bay. Napoleon returned to France and set about making himself ole leader in place of the committee, he Directoire, that ruled the country. It ell in 1799. Most people welcomed a trong ruler, and in 1802 Napoleon was nade First Consul. He brought in a new ode of laws, the Code Napoleon, mbodying some of the principles of the rench Revolution. In 1804 he had imself crowned emperor.

Napoleon enjoyed a string of uccesses on the battlefield against France's enemies: Prussia, Austria and Russia. He could not subdue Britain, however, and naval defeat by the British admiral Horatio Nelson at the battle of Trafalgar in 1805 ended his hopes of invasion. In 1807 he led his army through Spain to invade Portugal, and made his brother king of Spain. Britain responded by sending troops, beginning the long Peninsular War.

⌃ This map shows the French empire under Napoleon I and the main battles of the Napoleonic Wars.

In 1812 Napoleon led his Grand Army into Russia, but was driven back by the bitter Russian winter. By 1813 the French empire was collapsing. Napoleon abdicated as emperor in 1814. Escaping from exile on Elba, he raised a new army and made a final effort to win a victory and secure a peace. Defeat at Waterloo in 1815 ended his hopes, and he was exiled to Saint Helena, where he died in 1821.

▶ A caricature of the Duke of Wellington (who had a boot named after him). He led the British army in Spain and Portugal, and defeated Napoleon at Waterloo, in what is now Belgium.

| 806 | 1807 | 1808 | 1809 | 1812 | 1814 | 1815 |
|---|---|---|---|---|---|---|
| apoleon's rmy efeats the ussians : Jena. | Napoleon's army defeats the Russians at Friedland. France controls Portugal. | The Peninsular War starts when Napoleon puts his brother Joseph on the throne of Spain. | Napoleon marries the Austrian emperor's daughter, Marie Louise. | Napoleon's army invades Russia, but is defeated by the winter weather. In Spain the French army is defeated at Salamanca. | Napoleon is forced to abdicate and is exiled to the island of Elba, off Italy. | Napoleon escapes from Elba. He is defeated finally at the battle of Waterloo. |

# The Industrial Revolution

THE INDUSTRIAL Revolution began in Britain in the mid-18th century. Society was transformed as people moved from the countryside to the towns to work in factories.

The *Rocket*, designed and built in England, was the first intercity steam locomotive (1830)

of an improved steam engine, used for pumping water out of coal mines. It was now possible to produce more coal and better quality iron for industry.

TWO EVENTS in the early 18th century helped make the Industrial Revolution possible. The first was Abraham Darby's discovery that coke was a better fuel than charcoal for smelting iron. The second was Thomas Newcomen's invention

Until the 1760s most goods were hand-made by people working at home or in small workshops. Metalworkers made nails, pins and knives, and spinner and weavers produced woollen and

The first public railway, from Stockton to Darlington in England, opened in 1825. From 1830, steam locomotives were used to draw covered passenger carriages.

| 1698 | 1709 | 1712 | 1733 | 1742 | 1764 | 1769 |
|------|------|------|------|------|------|------|
| Thomas Savery develops a steam engine to pump water out of mines. | Abraham Darby discovers smelting iron with coke. | Thomas Newcomen improves the steam engine. | John Kay invents the flying shuttle, speeding up weaving. | First cotton factories in England. | James Hargreaves invents the spinning jenny. | James Watt designs a more efficient steam engine. Richard Arkwright invents a spinning frame powered by water. Josiah Wedgwood makes pottery. |

## SPINNING JENNY

James Hargreaves, inventor of the spinning jenny, was a poor spinner. He named his new machine after his daughter Jenny. Other hand-spinners feared his machines would put them out of work, and destroyed them.

linen cloth. But the 1700s saw a rising demand for cotton cloth, which at first was imported from India. Then raw cotton was imported, for manufacture into cloth in Britain.

In 1733 the invention of a flying shuttle speeded up the weaving process so much that spinning wheels could not produce enough yarn to keep the weavers supplied. Then, in 1764, James Hargreaves invented the spinning jenny, which allowed one person to spin eight threads at once. This was followed five years later by Richard Arkwright's heavy spinning frame, which was powered by water. Factories were built near fast-flowing streams to house these new machines, and the cotton industry boomed. By 1790, James Watt's improvements to the steam engine

meant that steam power could be used to drive machinery. This also increased the demand for coal to heat the water to make steam, and for iron to make the engines and other machinery. Canals (and later railways) were built to bring raw materials to the factories and take finished goods away. Towns grew rapidly, but housing and working conditions were often very poor and many people suffered from hunger, disease or accidents at work.

Pit machinery at an English coal mine in 1792. In the centre is a steam pump used to drain water from the mine. Steam engines were used to power machinery in factories too.

Children from the age of five up worked in coal mines. Some pulled heavy loads; others sat all day in darkness, opening and closing doors to let the air circulate.

| 1779 | 1799 | 1811 | 1815 | 1825 | 1842 |
|------|------|------|------|------|------|
| The first iron bridge is built. | Steam engines power mills making paper, flour and textiles. | Start of "Luddite" protests against new machinery. | Humphry Davy invents a safety lamp that warns miners of explosive gas. | First passenger railway in England (Stockton to Darlington). | The British parliament bans all women and children under the age of ten working underground in coal mines. |

# Europe in Turmoil

IN 1815, at the end of the Napoleonic Wars, Europe was in disorder. Old governments, with old ideas, were restored, but a new age of industrialism and democracy was dawning. At first people's demands for change were either ignored or crushed. Revolution seemed the only weapon to people all across Europe who still had no say in how they were governed.

These were the main centres of unrest in 1848, the "Year of Revolutions". By the end of 1849 all the revolts had been quashed.

REVOLT broke out in France in 1830, when Louis-Philippe was chosen as a "citizen-king" to replace the unpopular Charles X. Newspapers helped to spread reports of the uprising, sparking off protests in other countries. Within two years, Greece declared its independence

from Turkish rule, and Belgium from the Netherlands.

In 1848 so many revolutions and protests broke out again throughout Europe that it was known as the "Year of Revolutions". In Britain the Chartists demonstrated for political reforms and votes for all men. In France a group of rioters in Paris, who were demanding votes for all men and a new republic, were shot by soldiers. In Belgium, Denmark and the Netherlands reforms were made peacefully.

In Germany, many people wanted all the German states to be united into one country, and Italians wanted a united Italy. In contrast, in the vast Austrian empire the many groups of people who had their own languages wanted the empire to be divided into separate states to reflect this.

◀ The revolutions of 1848 started with a small revolt in Sicily (20 Jan). This inspired a revolt in France on 24 February. Soon the spirit of protest had spread across Europe.

◀ Riots broke out in Berlin in 1848. Men, women and children were attacked by Prussian soldiers as demands for reform and a united Germany were crushed.

The revolutions in 1848 were crushed by the end of 1849. The ideas that drove them did not go away, however. Many governments realized that they would have to make some reforms. Reformers looked for new ways of governing and distributing wealth more fairly. The German socialists Karl Marx and Friedrich Engels published their ideas in *The Communist Manifesto* in 1848. This was to have a huge impact on future events.

▶ Irishman Feargus O'Connor (1794–1855) was elected to the British parliament in 1832. He agitated for votes for all men, and led the Chartists from 1841 until 1848.

| 1831 | 1832 | 1838 | 1844 | 1848 | 1852 |
|---|---|---|---|---|---|
| Belgium declares independence from the Netherlands. | Greece becomes independent from the Ottoman empire. | In Britain, the People's Charter is published to demand political reforms. Its supporters become known as Chartists. | Friedrich Engels makes a study of the lives of workers in Manchester, England. | The Year of Revolutions affects most of Europe. | In France, the Second Republic is replaced by the Second Empire. |

# The British Empire

QUEEN VICTORIA came to the British throne in 1837 and reigned until her death in 1901. During her long reign, Britain became the world's most powerful nation, ruling a huge empire. The British Empire later evolved into the modern Commonwealth of independent nations.

Queen Victoria (1819–1901) was or 18 when she became queen. She took a keen interest in Britain's empire, and was delighted to become Empress of India in 1876.

MUCH OF BRITAIN'S WEALTH came from her colonies. Colonies and trading posts had been established in the 17th and 18th centuries in places as far apart as Canada, India, Australia and the Caribbean.

More were added by the Treaty of Vienn at the end of the Napoleonic Wars. Durin Victoria's reign, still more colonies were added, including New Zealand, many islands in the Pacific and Atlantic oceans parts of the Far East and large areas of Africa. At its greatest extent, in the late 19th century, the empire contained a quarter of the world's land and a quarter of its people.

The British Empire often featured in advertisements. This poster (for a warm drink) played on patriotic feeling during the Boer Wars (1899–1902).

## THE CRIMEAN WAR

During the Crimean War (1853–1856), Turkey, France and Britain fought against Russia. Thousands of British soldiers died from neglect and disease. Florence Nightingale and her team of nurses cleaned up the military hospitals and set up Britain's first training school for nurses.

| 1763 | 1788 | 1808 | 1815 | 1829 | 1830 | 1839–1842 | 1840 |
|---|---|---|---|---|---|---|---|
| Britain takes control of Canada. | First British settlement in Australia. | Sierra Leone becomes a British colony. | Treaty of Vienna gives Cape Colony (South Africa), Ceylon (Sri Lanka), Mauritius, Malta and French islands in the Caribbean to Britain. | Britain claims the whole of Australia. | Britain starts to control the Gold Coast (Ghana). | Britain fights Opium Wars to open China to trade. | By the Treaty Waitangi Br gains New Zealand. |

▶ The British Empire grew throughout the 19th century. The largest empire the world had ever seen was called "the empire on which the sun never sets".

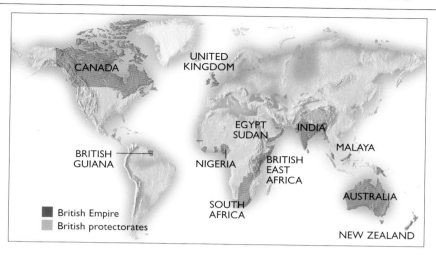

The colonies provided raw materials for British factories and a market for their goods. Some were at first run by trading companies, such as the East India Company in India. But gradually they all came under direct rule from Britain. In many colonies plantations were set up to produce tea, sugar, coffee, spices, rubber and cotton.

☑ Indian ports such as Madras and Calcutta became important centres of imperial trade.

The empire affected the lives of millions of people. British laws, technology and culture were taken all over the world. The British navy defended the empire. By 1900, however, Britain was no longer supreme as an industrial power, and the empire began to break up as countries sought independence.

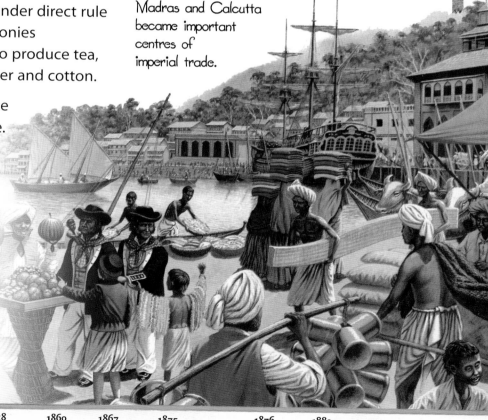

| 1843 | 1853–1856 | 1857–1858 | 1860 | 1867 | 1875 | 1876 | 1882 | 1901 |
|---|---|---|---|---|---|---|---|---|
| In West Africa, the Gambia becomes a British colony. | The Crimean War. | The Indian Mutiny leads to India being ruled directly from Britain. | Lagos (Nigeria) is added to the empire. | Canada becomes a British dominion. | Britain buys shares in the Suez Canal Company to control the trade route to India. | Victoria is crowned Empress of India. | Britain controls Egypt. | Death of Queen Victoria. |

# The American Civil War

CIVIL WAR between the Northern and Southern states split the United States of America and left a legacy of bitterness. The war was fought to end slavery, and to prevent the South breaking away from the Union.

Through his determination to win, Ulysses S Grant (1822–1885) led the Union armies to victory. He was President of the United States from 1869 to 1877.

THE NORTHERN states had the biggest cities and the most factories. Slavery there was banned by 1820, but in the Southern states, which had little industry, plantations relied on large numbers of slave-workers. Here slave-owning was accepted. In 1861 Abraham Lincoln was elected President. He pledged to end slavery in the United States. Many Southerners saw this as a threat to their way of life and in 1861 eleven Southern states announced that they were breaking away from the Union to form their own Confederacy. When the government told them they had no right to do this, civil war broke out.

The 23 Union (Northern) states had more soldiers and more money than the Confederacy, as well as the industry to provide weapons and supplies for war. With control of the navy, they were able to blockade Southern ports, cutting off supplies to the South from abroad, and preventing the export of cotton – a major source of wealth to the South.

The early battles were won by the South, but in July 1863 Union troops

## A NEW KIND OF WARFARE

The American Civil War was fought with new weapons, such as quick-loading rifles, ironclad (armoured) ships, submarines and even balloons (for observing enemy movements). Railways and telegraphs speeded up communications. Faced with deadly gunfire, soldiers were killed in large numbers as they tried to attack across open ground.

At the battle of Bull Run, Virginia, 1861, Confederate forces (right) led by Generals "Stonewall" Jackson and Beauregard defeated the Union army (left). It was the first major battle of the Civil War.

**1861**
Civil War starts when Confederate troops attack the Union garrison at Fort Sumter, South Carolina.

## GENERAL ROBERT E LEE

Before the war, Robert E Lee (1807–1870) was offered the command of the Union army by Lincoln, but turned it down when Virginia (his home state) withdrew from the Union. He became commander in chief of the Confederate army.

▶ In 1863 Abraham Lincoln (1809–1865) gave his famous Gettysburg Address and announced the abolition of slavery throughout the United States. This was approved by Congress in 1865.

defeated Confederate forces at the Battle of Gettysburg, Pennsylvania. Another Union army captured Vicksburg, Mississippi. In April 1865 the Confederate general Robert E Lee surrendered at Appomattox, Virginia. By this time, much of the South was in ruins. Over 600,000 soldiers died, more than half from disease. Five days after the surrender, Lincoln was assassinated. Though the war was over and slaves were set free, conditions for them hardly improved.

**1862**
Confederate General Lee prevents Union army taking Richmond, Virginia, and defeats another Union army at Fredericksburg, Virginia.

**1863**
Emancipation Proclamation is signed. Lee is defeated at Gettysburg, Pennsylvania.

**1864**
Grant's Union forces besiege Lee's forces at Petersburg, Virginia. Union General Sherman captures Atlanta and Savannah, Georgia.

**1865**
Grant's forces capture Richmond, Virginia. On 9 April, Lee surrenders to Grant at Appomattox, Virginia, bringing the war to an end. On 15 April, Lincoln is shot in a theatre by actor and Confederate sympathizer John Wilkes Booth.

# Unification of Italy

IN THE EARLY 1800s, Italy was united under the control of Napoleon. After Napoleon's defeat in 1815, Italy's states were handed back to their former rulers. Only Piedmont–Sardinia stayed independent.

OF THE ITALIAN states' foreign rulers, Austria was the most powerful. During the 1820s, opposition to foreign rule grew. The "Risorgimento" movement encouraged people to campaign for an independent, united Italy. Revolutions broke out in many states in 1848, but were crushed. In 1858, Piedmont–Sardinia allied itself with France and defeated Austria. This was followed in

1860 by a successful revolt led by Giuseppe Garibaldi and his army of "Redshirts". Garibaldi conquered Sicily, then Naples. Meanwhile, the northern states had joined up with Piedmont–Sardinia and accepted Victor Emmanuel II as their king. Garibaldi handed Naples and Sicily to him in November 1860 and in 1861 Italy was declared a kingdom.

🔽 The unification of Italy took 10 years. The last region to join was that of the Papal States, which surrounds Rome. Rome became the national capital in 1871.

▶ Giuseppe Garibaldi (1807– 1882), leader of the "Redshirts", agreeing to hand over the Kingdom of the Two Sicilies to Victor Emmanuel in 1860.

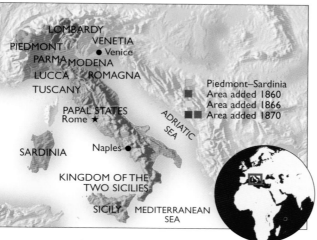

LOMBARDY
PIEDMONT VENETIA
● Venice
PARMA MODENA
LUCCA ROMAGNA
TUSCANY

Piedmont–Sardinia
Area added 1860
Area added 1866
Area added 1870

PAPAL STATES
Rome ★

ADRIATIC SEA

SARDINIA    Naples ●

KINGDOM OF THE TWO SICILIES

SICILY    MEDITERRANEAN SEA

| 1815 | From 1820s | 1848 | 1849 | 1852 | 1860 | 1861 | 1866 | 1871 |
|---|---|---|---|---|---|---|---|---|
| The Italian states are given back to their former rulers. | The Risorgimento – secret societies are formed to oppose foreign rule. | Unsuccessful revolutions in many states try to bring about unification. | Victor Emmanuel II becomes king of Piedmont–Sardinia. | Count Camillo Cavour unifies northern Italy. | Garibaldi and his Redshirts set out to conquer the Kingdom of the Two Sicilies. | Victor Emmanuel II becomes king of a unified Italy. | Venice becomes part of Italy. | Rome becomes part of Italy. |

# Unification of Germany

GERMANY, like Italy, was made up of separate states in the early 1800s. In 1815, after Napoleon's defeat, 38 states joined together as the German Confederation. Austria and Prussia were the two most powerful states to join.

Otto von Bismarck (1815–1898) went to war with Austria and France so that he could unite the north German states and make Prussia the ruler of a united Germany.

FROM THE START, Austria and Prussia competed against each other for leadership of the Confederation, and in 1866 Prussia declared war on Austria. After Prussia won a battle at Sadowa on the Elbe river, Otto von Bismarck, the chief Prussian minister, set up a separate North German Confederation dominated by Prussia.

In 1851 Napoleon III (1808–1873) declared himself emperor of France. He transformed Paris and encouraged industry. After the Franco-Prussian War his empire collapsed and he went into exile.

The French, threatened by the growing power of Prussia, declared war in 1870. Napoleon III's army of 100,000 men was heavily defeated at the battle of Sedan, however, and Napoleon III was taken prisoner. The people of Paris rose up against him and the French Second Empire was overthrown. The Prussian army then besieged Paris.

When the Franco-Prussian War ended on 10 May 1871, Germany had taken control of Alsace and Lorraine from the French. The German Second Empire was declared, with William II, king of Prussia, as emperor and Otto von Bismarck as chancellor.

This map shows the extent of the German Confederation in 1815. It included much of the old Holy Roman Empire (in red).

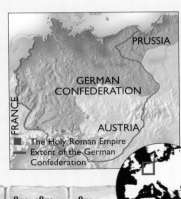

PRUSSIA

GERMAN CONFEDERATION

FRANCE

AUSTRIA

■ The Holy Roman Empire
Extent of the German Confederation

| 1815 | 1862 | 1864 | 1866 | 1870–1871 | 1871 |
|---|---|---|---|---|---|
| 38 German states form the German Confederation. | Bismarck becomes Prussia's foreign minister. He determines to make Prussia the most powerful state in the German Confederation. | Austria and Prussia declare war on Denmark and seize Schleswig-Holstein. | Prussia defeats Austria in the Seven Weeks' War. Venice is taken from Austria and given to Italy. | The Franco-Prussian War is won by Prussia. | Creation of the German Second Empire, ruled by William II, the former king of Prussia. |

# Scramble for Africa

IN 1880, less than five per cent of the African continent was ruled by European powers. Most European nations had been content with trading colonies around the coast. Only the British and the Boers in South Africa had moved inland and set up new settlements. But within 20 years the situation changed completely, in what is known as the Scramble for Africa.

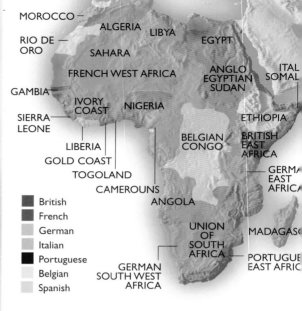

MOROCCO
RIO DE ORO
ALGERIA
LIBYA
EGYPT
SAHARA
FRENCH WEST AFRICA
ANGLO EGYPTIAN SUDAN
ITAL SOMAL
GAMBIA
IVORY COAST
NIGERIA
SIERRA LEONE
ETHIOPIA
LIBERIA
BELGIAN CONGO
BRITISH EAST AFRICA
GOLD COAST
TOGOLAND
GERMA EAST AFRICA
CAMEROUNS
ANGOLA
UNION OF SOUTH AFRICA
MADAGAS
GERMAN SOUTH WEST AFRICA
PORTUGUE EAST AFRIC

- British
- French
- German
- Italian
- Portuguese
- Belgian
- Spanish

In 1914, European powers had control of most of Africa. Only two countries were independent: Ethiopia and Liberia.

SEVEN EUROPEAN nations took control of the whole of Africa, apart from Liberia and Ethiopia. By 1884 Belgium, Britain, France, Portugal and Spain had started to claim new colonies in Africa or expand their old ones. The newly unified countries of Germany and Italy also wanted shares of the continent. To prevent serious conflict, the European

At Isandhlwana in southern Africa, the Zulus fought the British, killing 1,700 British soldiers at the start of the Zulu War in 1879. Later the Zulus were themselves defeated.

| 1880 | 1882 | 1884 | 1889 | 1890 | 1891 | 1893 |
|---|---|---|---|---|---|---|
| Leopold II, king of Belgium, claims the Congo as his own personal territory. | Britain takes control of Egypt to secure access to the Suez Canal. | Conference of Berlin divides Africa among seven European countries. | The British conquer the Matabele and take their land, calling it Rhodesia. | The Italians take Eritrea and try, but fail, to conquer Abyssinia (now Ethiopia). | Tanganyika (now Tanzania) becomes a German protectorate. The French make northern Algeria part of France. | The French take control of Mali. |

owers met at an international onference on Africa held in Berlin. he conference allowed the uropeans to divide Africa, with little egard for the African peoples, their ultures or their natural boundaries. esistance by black Africans, or indeed by hite Boers in southern Africa, was rushed by well-equipped European rmies. Thousands of Africans died in the ghting, and others suffered hardship nd hunger as their traditional ways of fe were destroyed. Some were forced to vork as cheap labour in mines and on lantations, growing cotton, tea, coffee nd cocoa for export to Europe. uropeans started farms in suitable areas, nd built roads and railways.

In the better-run European olonies, schools and medical entres were set up for local eople. In the worst-run olonies, African people were eated little better than slaves. nder European rule, Africans ained access to new ideas, ut had no say in how their ves were run.

## CECIL RHODES

British-born Cecil Rhodes (1853–1902) went to Natal in southern Africa when he was 17 years old. He became a member of the Cape Colony parliament in 1881 and prime minister in 1890. Rhodes helped to bring more territory under British control, but failed in his ambition to give Britain an empire in Africa that extended from the Cape to Egypt.

On the Great Trek during the 1830s, many Boers left Cape Colony and headed north to escape British rule.

# The Modern World

## INTO A NEW MILLENNIUM
### 1900–2000s

WHEN the 20th century began, large areas of the world were controlled by European powers, including Britain, France and Germany. China and Russia lagged behind in industrial might. The new power in Asia was Japan, while the United States was fast becoming the world's industrial giant. During the 1900s, the tide of power ebbed and flowed, but overall the 20th century was dominated by the wealth and culture of the United States.

IT WAS A CENTURY of rapid change in society, in science and technology, and in everyday life. It was the age of aircraft, television, space rockets, computers and genetic engineering. The world's population increased dramatically to over six billion people. Many of these people were poor and hungry, while others living in rich countries enjoyed comforts and entertainments unimaginable in earlier times.

Everywhere people demanded equal rights. There were revolutions in many countries. The revolution in Russia in 1917 made some people believe that Communism was the new

| 1914–1918 | 1917 | 1929 | 1933 | 1936–1939 | 1939–1945 | 1947 | 1948 |
|---|---|---|---|---|---|---|---|
| World War I sees more than 8.5 million soldiers killed. | The Russian Revolution starts when the Bolsheviks, led by Lenin, seize power. They gain control of all of Russia by 1921. | The Wall Street Crash sparks the Great Depression. | Nazis, led by Adolf Hitler, come to power in Germany. | Spanish Civil War. | World War II. The USA enters the war in 1941. In 1945 Germany and Japan surrender. | Pakistan and India gain independence from Britain. | Israel is founded. First Arab-Israeli war. |

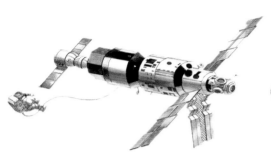

rld order. Anti-Communist revolutions eastern Europe in the 1980s and 1990s owed this was not so. There were two rld wars (1914–1918 and 1939–1945), d many smaller wars. World War I ded in defeat for Germany and its es, but the peace that followed was an easy one and did not last long. World r II was the most costly war of all time, d the most horrific.

By 1950, the United States was the ongest power, for a while challenged the Communist Soviet Union in what came known as the Cold War. Europe, dly damaged by war, reshaped itself as European Union. Japan modernized d became an industrial powerhouse.

Old empires ended, and new alliances were made. New independent nations, including India and the new nations of Africa, joined the United Nations. China emerged from years of isolation.

New communications such as the Internet, satellite TV and world tourism made the world seem smaller. Problems in one country often affected others. Global concerns, such as the threat to the tropical rainforests or fast-dwindling oil supplies, could not be contained within national borders. Terrorism became a new threat to peace. So fast was the pace of change that it is hard to predict what the world will be like when the 21st century draws to a close.

| | 1960s | 1965–1975 | 1969 | 1990 | 1991 | 1994 | 2001 |
|---|---|---|---|---|---|---|---|
| munists y Mao ng gain ol of a. | Most countries in Africa gain independence from colonial rule. | The Vietnam War. | US astronaut Neil Armstrong is first to walk on the Moon. | East and West Germany are reunited. | The Soviet Union collapses and the Cold War ends. | Free elections in South Africa. | Terrorists crash airliners into the World Trade Center in New York City and the Pentagon in Washington DC. US-led forces invade Afghanistan to remove Taliban government. |

# World War I

WORLD WAR I began as a European quarrel, caused by rivalry between nations. It spread to the oceans, to the Middle East and to Africa. The war cost the lives of more than 8 million soldiers, many killed in awful trench warfare. The war was so frightful that afterwards people said it had been the Great War, "the war to end wars". It was not.

⌃ On the Western Front most of the fightin took place in northern France and Belgium. Mules and horses were used to bring supplies and heavy guns to the front.

BETWEEN 1880 and 1907, the European powers had formed alliances and increased their armies and navies. On o side stood the Allies: Britain, France, Russia and Japan. On the other were th Central Powers: Germany, Austria-Hungary, Turkey and Serbia. Italy later joined the Allies. The spark that started

⌄ In the trenches soldiers ate and slept while waiting for orders to go into battle. Dug-outs, or underground shelters, offered some protection from enemy shells, but the trenches were usually cold, muddy and wet.

| 1914, 28 June | 1914, 28 July–3 August | 1914, 4 August | 1914, 26 August | 1914, September | 1914, November |
|---|---|---|---|---|---|
| A Serb, Gavrilo Princip, assassinates Archduke Franz Ferdinand in Sarajevo. | Austria declares war on Serbia. Russia prepares to defend Serbia. Germany declares war on Russia, then on France. | German armies march through Belgium to France. Britain declares war on Germany. World War I begins. | Germany defeats Russian forces at the battle of Tannenberg. | At the battle of the Marne the Allies halt the German advance on Paris. | At the end of the battle of Ypres German forces are prevented from reaching the Channel. |

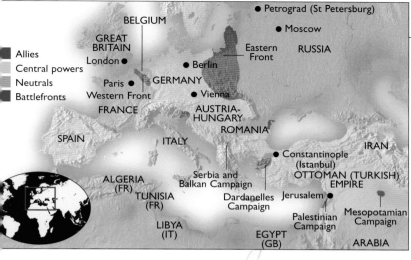

◄ The war in Europe was fought on the Western Front, between France and Germany, and the Eastern Front, from the Baltic towards the Black Sea. There was also fighting in the Middle East, the Italy–Austria border, and in Africa.

...he war was the assassination of ...ustrian Archduke Franz Ferdinand by a ...erb in June 1914. This led to a series of ...obilizations (preparing for war), and on ... August German armies invaded ...elgium. This drew Britain, Belgium's ally ...ince 1830, into the war.

World War I was fought mostly on ...nd (there was only one big naval ...attle, at Jutland in 1916). Both sides got ...ogged down in trench warfare, their ...rmies unable to advance without ...uge losses. Soldiers had to go "over ...he top" (leave the trench), scramble ...hrough their own barbed-wire ...efences, then cross open ground ("no-...an's land") to reach the enemy lines. So ...uick and powerful were the machine ...uns and heavy artillery guns that ...oldiers were killed in their thousands. In

the battle of the Somme alone (1916), there were over a million casualties.

By 1917, Russia was so weak that it began peace talks with Germany. For a while Germany had an advantage, but in 1918 the arrival of more than a million US soldiers boosted the Allies, who began to advance. There were food shortages and unrest in Germany, and emperor Wilhelm II abdicated. On 11 November, an armistice was signed between Germany and the Allies, ending the war.

WAR PLANES
World War I (1914–1918) was the first war in which aeroplanes were widely used. They were first used to spy on enemy trenches and troop movements. Later, they were used in aerial combat and in bombing raids.

| 1915, April–May | 1915, 22 May | 1916 February | 1916, 1 July | 1917 | 1917, July | 1918 March 3 | 1918, November |
|---|---|---|---|---|---|---|---|
| ...ermany uses ...ison gas for ...st time at ...cond battle ... Ypres. | Italy joins the Allies. | Start of battle for Verdun, France, lasting for five months. | Start of the battle of the Somme, France; ends in November. | On April 6 the USA joins the war on the Allied side. | Third battle of Ypres (Passchendaele). | Cease-fire between Russia and Germany. | Armistice is signed on 11 November at 11 o'clock. World War I ends. |

# The Russian Revolution

IN THE 19TH century, efforts to modernize Russia by freeing the serfs (peasants), building factories and introducing democracy came to nothing. Tsar Alexander II made reforms, but in 1881 he was assassinated. Tsar Alexander III undid most of his father's work, and in desperation some Russians turned to revolution.

THE FIRST SERIOUS rebellion broke out in 1905, after troops fired on striking workers in the capital, St Petersburg. The rebellion was soon crushed and the leaders, including Lenin, went into exile. The new tsar, Nicholas II, promised the people more civil rights, but the promise was soon broken.

When World War I started, life for most people in Russia went from bad to worse. The railways no longer carried food, fuel and supplies to the cities. The economy almost collapsed and people went hungry. In March 1917 riots broke out again. This time the troops joined the rioters. Nicholas abdicated and his advisers resigned.

A temporary government was set up, led by Alexander Kerensky, but unrest continued. The Bolsheviks, led by Lenin, planned a take-over. In November they attacked the Winter Palace in St Petersburg and seized power (an event known as the October Revolution, because Russia used a different calendar at that time). The Bolsheviks

> Armed workers led by the Bolsheviks stormed St Petersburg's Winter Palace in 1917, starting the revolution. They were joined by Russian soldiers, tired of fighting the Germans in World War I.

Leon Trotsky (1879–1940), a leader of the Bolshevik revolution, was the most powerful man in Russia after Lenin. When Stalin came to power in 1924, he was exiled and later murdered.

Tsar Nicholas II with his wife Alexandra and their five children. After the revolution, they were all imprisoned, and in 1918 they were executed.

## LENIN

Vladimir Ilyich Ulyanor (1870–1924) used the name Lenin. He led the Bolsheviks from 1898, but was exiled from 1905 to 1917. On his return the Bolsheviks seized power and he became Russia's new leader.

> Many Russians blamed Rasputin (1869–1916) for persuading Tsar Nicholas II to ignore the people's complaints. Rasputin, a priest, claimed he had the power to heal the emperor's sick son.

moved the capital to Moscow and made peace with Germany. They broke up large estates and gave the land to the peasants. Workers took control of the factories and the state took control of the banks. In 1918 civil war broke out between the Bolshevik Red Army and anti-Communist

White Russians. This ended in victory for the Bolsheviks in 1921. The following year, the Union of Soviet Socialist Republics was formed. Lenin died in 1924, and was succeeded by Joseph Stalin. Stalin's rule was tyrannical. He had millions of people killed or sent to prison camps, where they died.

| 1887 | 1894 | 1905 | 1917 | 1918 | 1922 |
|---|---|---|---|---|---|
| Lenin becomes a Marxist. | Nicholas II becomes tsar. | Some 200,000 people march on the Winter Palace in St Petersburg. Lenin is exiled. | Lenin returns. Nicholas II abdicates and a republican government is formed. Revolutionaries attack the Winter Palace and the government falls. | Russia withdraws from World War I. The imperial family is executed. Civil war between the Red Army (Communists) and White Russians (anti-Communists) lasts until 1921. | The Russian empire is renamed the Union of Soviet Socialist Republics. |

# The Great Depression

AFTER World War I, the economies of many European countries were in ruins. Defeated Germany had to pay reparations (money as compensation for the war) to Britain and France. German money became worthless. By 1929, the whole world economy seemed to be falling apart. Millions of people lost money, jobs and homes.

On the Jarrow Crusade (1935) in England 200 men walked from Jarrow in northern England to London to draw attention to unemployment in their home town.

IN THE USA, whose banks had loaned money to other nations for the war, many people had invested savings in stocks. Buying pushed up prices of company shares beyond their real value. In August 1929 share prices started to fall, and people began to panic. They sold their shares, which made prices fall even faster. Many people lost all their savings in the Stock Market Crash. Banks and businesses closed and many people lost their jobs.

A severe drought in the American Midwest made things even worse. In the Dust Bowl, where fertile topsoil was worn away by over-farming, the drought and wind turned

Soup kitchens serving free food were set up in many citi to feed the hungry. It was estimated that over a quarter of the population of the USA relied on begging, charity handouts and limited public welfar

**1929**
In October the New York Stock Exchange on Wall Street crashes after people panic and sell their shares.

**1932**
At the height of the Depression there are 12,000,000 unemployed people in the USA. Franklin D Roosevelt is elected President.

he fields to dusty deserts.
Many farms were
abandoned as families
headed west to California.

The crisis in the USA
affected the world, as
money loaned overseas
by US banks was called

## THE NEW DEAL

Part of President Roosevelt's New
Deal in 1933 included a programme
to create more jobs. Young people
were given work in the national
forests, and a series of dams were
built on the Tennessee river to
provide electricity and prevent soil
erosion. New welfare and labour laws
improved working conditions.

back. Britain and Germany were hit
especially hard, and unemployment
rose rapidly. Jobless men lined up for
handouts of food and clothes.
Countries tried to protect their
industries by taxing foreign
goods. By 1932, when the
Depression reached its deepest,
world exports of raw materials
had fallen by over 70 per cent,
ruining the economies of poorer
countries that depended on selling
food and raw materials.

⌃ The New
York Stock Exchange on Wall Street, October
1929. As share prices fell, many investors
rushed to the Exchange to discover that they
had lost all their money.

▶ The Depression
brought misery for millions
of people who lost their
jobs. This chart shows
how unemployment soared
in 1932. It started to fall
as economies recovered.

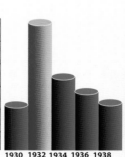

1930 1932 1934 1936 1938

33
oosevelt introduces the
ew Deal to protect people's
vings and create jobs. In
ermany there are
000,000 unemployed.

1935
In Britain 200 men march
from Jarrow to London with
a petition drawing
attention to
unemployment.

1936
The Depression ends
in Germany as public
works and weapons
production bring full
employment.

1939
About 15 per cent
of the workforce
in the USA is still
unemployed.

1941
Full employment
returns to the
USA as it enters
World War II.

# World War II

WORLD WAR II began on 3 September 1939, two days after German armies invaded Poland. When Germany's leader, Adolf Hitler, refused to withdraw his troops, Britain and France declared war. The war was fought between the Axis powers (chiefly Germany, Italy and Japan) and the Allies (who included Britain and its Commonwealth partners, France, the Soviet Union and the United States).

Winston Church (1874–1965) was prime minister of Britain from 1940 1945. He is seen here making his famo "V" for victory sign.

take-overs. By June 1940, most of Europe had fallen. Britain stood alone. In August and September, Hitler's air force, the Luftwaffe, attacked southeast England and London in daylight raids. Despite having fewer planes, the British air forc managed to fight off the German and so prevent an invasion Even so, many Britis towns and cities were bombed in the Bli attacks that followe

ON 17 SEPTEMBER, the Soviet Union invaded Poland from the east. By the end of 1939, Soviet troops had also invaded Estonia, Latvia, Lithuania and Finland. In the spring of 1940 German troops invaded Denmark, Norway, Belgium, the Netherlands and France. Using vast numbers of tanks and bomber planes, they swiftly overwhelmed defences – a tactic known as Blitzkrieg (German for "lightning war"). Infantry completed the

The Battle of Brita raged above souther England from August t October, 1940. RAF plane (right) fought off Germa planes (left). Over 2,600 aircraft were shot dow

| 1939 | 1939, 23 August | 1939, 25 August | 1939, 1 September | 1939, 3 September | 1939, 17 September | 1939, 17 December |
|---|---|---|---|---|---|---|
| Germany annexes Czechoslovakia. Italy annexes Albania. Italy and Germany form an alliance. | Germany and the USSR sign a non-aggression pact. | Britain, France and Poland form an alliance. | Germany invades Poland. | Britain and France declare war on Germany. | The USSR invades Poland. | The River Plate naval battle in South America. Germany loses the battleship *Graf Spree*. |

Under German control
Neutral countries

FINLAND
NORWAY
SWEDEN
NETHERLANDS
IRELAND
BRITAIN    DENMARK          RUSSIA
BELGIUM
GERMANY    POLAND
ORTUGAL    FRANCE    CZECHO-
SLOVAKIA
AUSTRIA
HUNGARY
YUGOSLAVIA  ROMANIA
SPAIN        ALBANIA
SWITZERLAND    BULGARIA
ITALY              TURKEY
GREECE
NORTH
AFRICA

◀ By the end of 1941, Germany controlled most of Europe and North Africa and part of Russia. In Europe, only neutral countries and Britain were still free.

forced the British back to the Egyptian border.

Encouraged by his successes, Hitler launched an attack on his former ally, the Soviet Union, in June 1941, invading the vast country with the help of Finland, Hungary and Romania. By the end of 1941, however, Allied fortunes were about to change as the USA joined the war, following the unprovoked attack on its navy at Pearl Harbor in Hawaii by the Japanese.

In September 1940, Italian troops moved into Egypt, where Britain had part of its army stationed to defend the Suez Canal. By February 1941, the Italians had been defeated, but German troops

▼ Many children from British cities were sent to live with families in the country, away from the bombs. They were evacuees.

| 940, larch | 1940, April–May | 1940, June | 1940, August– October | 1940, November |
|---|---|---|---|---|
| he USSR kes nland. | Germany occupies Norway, Denmark, Belgium and the Netherlands. | Germany occupies France. Allies evacuate from Dunkirk. | Battle of Britain. | Italy tries to invade Greece. Hungary, Romania and Slovakia join the Axis powers. |

# World at War

THE JAPANESE attack on the US naval base at Pearl Harbor brought the United States, with its industrial and military might, into the war. Before this, many Americans had supported Britain in its fight against Nazi Germany, but had been reluctant to get involved in a European war. Now it was different.

British general Bernard Montgomery (1887–1976) led the Allies to victory over German and Italian forces the North African desert.

MILLIONS OF US TROOPS were soon on their way to fight in Europe and the Pacific, and the USA threw its air force and navy into the battles against both Germany and Japan. USA guns, tanks and planes were shipped across the Atlantic Ocean to Britain, still suffering from German air raids and from shortages caused by German submarine attacks

on supply ships. The Allies began to bomb German cities, the British bombing by night while the Americans raided by day. They used ships and planes to hunt enemy submarines or U-boats.

By August 1941 the US forces in the Pacific had defeated the Japanese at the battles of the Coral Sea, Midway and Guadalcanal. These victories halted the Japanese advance. The USA used aircraft carriers against Japanese ships, and from captured island bases sent planes on bombing raids against Japan itself.

The US naval base at Pearl Harbor in Hawaii was attacked without warning by the Japanese air force on 7 December, 1941. Four battleships were destroyed, many more damaged and 3,300 people killed. This attack brought the USA into the war on the side of the Allies.

◀ German and Finnish forces besieged the Russian city of Leningrad (now St Petersburg) from 1941 to 1944. About one million people died of cold, hunger, disease and injury.

In Africa, British and Commonwealth troops won a decisive battle at El Alamein, Egypt, in late 1942. As the British advanced west across the desert, they trapped the enemy between more Allied forces advancing from Algeria and Morocco.

The North African battles were over by May 1943, and the Allies began plans for the invasion of Italy and France.

In Russia, German armies got to within sight of Moscow by November 1941, but were forced back. The Germans were beaten at Stalingrad (now Volgograd) in 1943, and retreated from Russia as the Soviet Red Army moved steadily west. The long-awaited "second front" in western Europe opened on 6 June, 1944, when Allied armies landed in Normandy, France.

▶ After bombing raids, rescuers battled fires and pulled out survivors. German planes bombed Britain during the Blitz. Later, Allied bombers destroyed homes and industrial plants in Germany and Japan. An Allied raid on the German city of Dresden in 1945 killed about 80,000 people.

**1942, October**
In North Africa, Allies defeat Axis forces at the battle of El Alamein, Egypt.

**1943, February**
The battle of Stalingrad ends in defeat for the Germans.

**1943, May**
Axis troops in North Africa surrender.

**1943, July**
Allied troops invade Sicily. Mussolini's government is overthrown and Italy declares war on Germany.

# Horror and Holocaust

THE WAR in Europe was over by May 1945, and the war in the Pacific by August. As the Allies liberated conquered countries and occupied Germany, they discovered the horrors of the Holocaust – the Nazi plan to round up and exterminate Jews.

Nagasaki (left) and Hiroshima in Japan were flattened in an instant by atomic bombs. Many people died later from radiation.

of German manufacturing and arms production. Meanwhile, Soviet troops were heading towards Berlin. Realizing he was facing defeat, Hitler committed suicide on 30 April. Soviet troops captured Berlin two days later. On 9 May, Germany officially surrendered.

THE ALLIED INVASION of Europe started on 6 June 1944. By 2 July, one million troops had landed in France. In March 1945 Allied troops crossed the river Rhine and in April they reached the Ruhr, the heartland

US B-17 bombers raided targets in Europe and Asia.

The Allies planned to invade Japan in late 1945, but feared heavy losses. On 6 August, 1945 an atomic bomb was dropped on the Japanese city of Hiroshima, and three days later a second bomb fell on Nagasaki. The Japanese surrendered, and on 14 August World War II was over.

Almost six years of war had cost 17 million lives and done enormous damage. Many casualties were civilians.

The Allied war leaders Churchill (left), Roosevelt and Stalin – the "Big Three" – met to plan the defeat of Germany and Japan.

| 1944 | 1944, June | 1944, July | 1944, December | 1945, February | 1945, March | 1945, April |
|---|---|---|---|---|---|---|
| Germans launch V-1 pilotless planes and V-2 rockets against England. | Allied forces land in Normandy, France, to start the liberation of Europe. | German plotters attempt to kill Hitler, but fail. | Start of battle of the Bulge, last German offensive in Europe. | At the Yalta Conference, Allies agree to divide Germany into four zones after the war. | US troops capture Iwo Jima island, in the Pacific. | Adolf Hitler kills himself. |

◄ Allied soldiers rescued sick and starved Holocaust survivors from Nazi death camps such as Belsen and Auschwitz. Millions of people had been killed in the camps.

### NUREMBERG TRIALS

After World War II, the Allies set up an international military court at Nuremberg in Germany to try the Nazi leaders for war crimes. Twelve were sentenced to death and six were sent to prison. Hermann Goering (above) committed suicide before his sentence could be carried out. Concentration camp commanders were also tried.

The Allies were shocked to learn of the ill-treatment of prisoners-of-war by the Japanese. In Germany, they saw the evidence of the Holocaust – concentration camps in which the Nazis had systematically murdered millions of Jews and other helpless victims. Around six million Jews had been starved, tortured or killed in gas chambers.

After the war, the USSR controlled most of eastern Europe. Germany was divided. War criminals were tried for crimes against humanity. As reconstruction began, the United Nations was formed to try to prevent future wars.

▼ The Allied invasion of Normandy began on 6 June, 1944 (D-Day). About 156,000 troops were landed in the largest seaborne attack ever mounted.

| 1945, May | 1945, June | 1945, August | 1945, October |
|---|---|---|---|
| Soviet troops enter Berlin. Germany surrenders. | US forces capture Okinawa island, close to Japan. | Atomic bombs dropped on Hiroshima and Nagasaki. Japan surrenders. | The United Nations is formed. |

# Israel and Palestine

THE ANCIENT homeland of the Jews was the land around Jerusalem. The Jews were later expelled and by the 20th century most Jews lived elsewhere, in Europe, the USA and Russia. The land, now called Palestine, had for many years been part of the Ottoman empire. The Jews' desire to return led to a long conflict with the people living there.

> Polish-born David Ben Gurion (1886–1973) emigrated to Palestine in 1906. Known as the Father of the Nation, he was Israel's first prime minister.

MOST Palestinians were Arabs. Small numbers of Jews, known as Zionists, began to settle in Palestine in the 1880s. In 1917, Britain declared its support for a Jewish homeland in Palestine. The Ottoman empire was breaking up following Turkey's defeat in World War I. The new League of Nations gave Britain its mandate (permission) to rule Palestine in the short term.

Jews continued to settle in Palestine, especially when in the 1930s the Nazis in Germany began to persecute German Jews. To escape imprisonment or murder, those Jews who could began to leave Germany. Some went to other European countries or to the USA.

< T E Lawrence (1888–1935), known as Lawrence of Arabia, was a British soldier who helped to lead an Arab revolt against the Ottoman empire during World War I. After that war, many Arabs hoped to see a new Arab nation, to include Palestine. This did not happen.

| 1840 | 1882 | 1917 | 1920 | 1922 | 1929 | 1933 | 1939 |
|---|---|---|---|---|---|---|---|
| After brief rule by Egypt, Palestine becomes part of the Ottoman empire again. | First Zionist settlement established in Palestine. | The Balfour Declaration supports a Jewish homeland in Palestine. | The Treaty of Sevres ends the Ottoman empire. | Britain is given the mandate to govern Palestine. | First major conflict between Jews and Arabs. | Persecution of the Jews begins in Germany. | Britain agrees to restrict the number of Jews emigrating to Palestine. |

others moved to Palestine. The growing numbers of immigrants led to fighting between Jews and Arabs, and Britain tried to restrict the numbers of settlers allowed in.

After World War II, many more Jews wanted to move to Palestine. Britain took the matter to the United Nations and in 1947 it was decided to split Palestine into two states, one Jewish and the other Arab. Jerusalem would become international, since it was sacred to Jews, Muslims and Christians. The Jews agreed to this, but the Arabs

Since 1948 Israeli defence forces have been on constant alert against attack. Israel's neighbours became its enemies, refusing to recognize the new Jewish state. In turn, Israel refused to acknowledge Palestinian land claims.

did not. Britain gave up its mandate on 14 May. 1948 and, on the same day, the Jewish leader David Ben Gurion announced the founding of the state of Israel. The Arab League (Syria, Lebanon, Iraq, Iran, Jordan and Egypt) declared war on Israel. Israel quickly defeated them, gaining more land.

The Wailing Wall in Jerusalem is a Jewish place of prayer. After 1948, the Wall was in the part of the city held by Jordan. Israel regained it in 1967 and claimed all Jerusalem as its capital. Finding a future for Jerusalem that satisfies all has proved very difficult.

Golda Meir (1898–1978) was Israel's prime minister from 1969 to 1974. Born in Russia, she lived in the USA as a child and moved to Palestine in 1921.

| 1947 | 1948 | 1949 |
|---|---|---|
| The United Nations votes to divide Palestine. | On 14 May the state of Israel is founded and the Arab League declares war. | A UN-negotiated cease-fire leaves Israel with the territory given to it in 1947. |

# The Cold War

THE USA and the Soviet Union emerged from World War II as the world's dominant superpowers. Former allies, they soon became enemies in what was known as the Cold War.

This cartoon shows Soviet leader Nikita Khruschev (on the left) and US president John F Kennedy arm-wrestling on top of nuclear missiles. In 1962 a clash of the two superpowers was avoided only when Soviet ships (above) carrying rockets to Cuba turned back.

THE COLD WAR started when the Soviet Union set up Communist governments in the countries of Eastern Europe liberated by the Red Army. This effectively divided Europe by an "iron curtain". To stop Communism spreading to the West, the US-backed Marshall Plan was set up to give financial aid to countries whose economies had been ruined by the war.

The Berlin Wall was built across the city in 1961 to divide the eastern part from the west, and so prevent people escaping from Communist rule.

After the war Germany was divided between the Allies. The USA, Britain and France controlled the west of the country, while the east was controlled by the Soviet Union. The capital, Berlin, lay within Soviet-controlled territory, but was also divided. In 1948 the Soviets tried to blockade West Berlin, forcing the Allies to airlift in supplies. In 1949 Germany was divided into West and East.

| 1947 | 1948 | 1949 | 1950–1953 | 1953 | 1955 | 1956 |
|---|---|---|---|---|---|---|
| The US-backed Marshall Plan gives financial aid to European countries. | Blockade of West Berlin for five months by the Soviet Union. | North Atlantic Treaty Organization (NATO) is formed. Communists come to power in mainland China. | The Korean War. North Korea, supported by China, invades South Korea, supported by the USA. | Death of Joseph Stalin. | Warsaw Pact formed among countries of Eastern Europe. | Soviets invade Hungary to preserve Communist rule. |

NATO countries
Warsaw Pact
Neutral countries

NORWAY  FINLAND
SWEDEN
NETHERLANDS  SOVIET UNION
IRELAND
BRITAIN  DENMARK
EAST
GERMANY
WEST  POLAND
GERMANY  CZECHOSLOVAKIA
PORTUGAL  FRANCE  AUSTRIA
HUNGARY
SWITZERLAND  ROMANIA
YUGOSLAVIA
SPAIN  BULGARIA
ITALY  ALBANIA
TURKEY
GREECE

◀ This map shows how Europe was divided after World War II. The boundary between democratic (pink) and Communist (red) Europe was first named the "iron curtain" by Winston Churchill.

Both sides built up huge stocks of nuclear weapons. This led to another crisis in 1962, when Cuban dictator Fidel Castro allowed the Soviet Union to build missile bases in Cuba, close to the USA. US President John F Kennedy ordered the US Navy to blockade Cuba, and eventually the Soviets agreed to

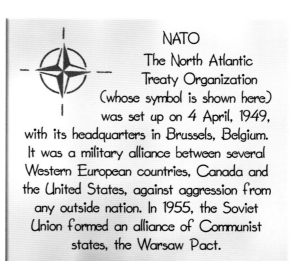

withdraw. To prevent a nuclear war from starting, the missiles were removed.

The two sides in the Cold War spent vast sums on weapons. Although they never fought directly, they did get involved in the Korean War in the 1950s and the Vietnam War in the 1960s and 1970s. They also carried on a spying and propaganda campaign against one another for many years. Any moves towards freedom in Communist Europe were crushed by the Soviet Union.

▲ In 1968, Prague, the Czech capital, was invaded by Soviet tanks. A new Czech government had brought in reforms that were feared by the Soviet Communist leaders.

NATO
The North Atlantic Treaty Organization (whose symbol is shown here) was set up on 4 April, 1949, with its headquarters in Brussels, Belgium. It was a military alliance between several Western European countries, Canada and the United States, against aggression from any outside nation. In 1955, the Soviet Union formed an alliance of Communist states, the Warsaw Pact.

| 1958 | 1960 | 1961 | 1962 | 1963 | 1964 | 1968 |
|---|---|---|---|---|---|---|
| Fidel Castro comes to power in Cuba and allies Cuba with the Soviet Union. | A split develops between the Soviet Union and China. | The Berlin Wall is built. | Cuban missile crisis. | The USA and the Soviet Union sign a Nuclear Test-Ban Treaty. | The USA becomes involved in the Vietnam War. | Invasion of Czechoslovakia by the Soviet Union to preserve Communist rule. |

# Fight for Rights

DURING the second half of the 20th century, people all over the world fought for civil rights. Many were being treated unfairly because of their race, skin colour, religion or gender. Others were being denied the vote, barred from forming free trade unions, or prevented from choosing the political leaders they wanted.

Polish workers protest. *Solidarity* was a trade union started in the shipyards of Gdansk, Poland, in 1980. It campaigned for workers' rights and led to an anti-Communist movement.

THE CIVIL RIGHTS movement came to the fore in the USA in the 1960s. In the southern states, blacks were discriminated against in schools, jobs, transport and health care. Protests began in 1955, after Rosa Parks, a black American, was arrested for refusing to give up her seat to a white man on a bus in Alabama. Non-violent protests were inspired by the words of Civil Rights leader Dr Martin Luther King. He led a march to Washington, DC, in 1963. Over 250,000 people took part, and in 1964 the US government passed a Civil Rights Act that made racial discrimination illegal.

Martin Luther King (1929–1968) was an outstanding speaker. His belief in non-violent resistance to oppression won him the Nobel peace prize in 1964. His most famous speech included the words: "I have a dream". In 1968 King was shot dead in Memphis, Tennessee.

| 1955 | 1957 | 1960 | 1962 | 1963 | 1964 | 1966 |
|---|---|---|---|---|---|---|
| Rosa Parks is arrested in Alabama for refusing to give up her seat on a bus. | In the USA, Martin Luther King brings many civil rights groups together. | South African police fire on anti-Apartheid demonstrators at Sharpeville, killing 69. | Nelson Mandela is imprisoned for political activities. | Martin Luther King organizes a march to Washington, DC, asking for equal rights for all. | The Civil Rights Act is passed in the USA to end all discrimination because of race, colour, religion or national origin. | American feminists found the National Organization for Women. |

There was a similar struggle in South Africa, where the white minority government's policy of apartheid (separating the races) was oppressive and cruel. After 69 African protesters were shot dead at Sharpeville in 1969, the campaign became more violent. Black leader Nelson Mandela was jailed from 1962 until 1990. After a long international campaign of protest and sanctions against South Africa, Mandela was released from prison and apartheid ended in 1990.

## APARTHEID

Apartheid means "apartness". It was a policy used in South Africa from 1948 to 1990 to divide the country into separate areas for whites and blacks. There was segregated education, employment, housing and health care. Most whites had good jobs and lived in comfort; blacks did the heavy work and lived in crowded townships.

In Communist countries, people demanded the right to form free trade unions and to vote for whatever kind of government they wanted. Women campaigned for equal pay and job opportunities. New laws in some countries banned sex and age discrimination in employment.

▶ Nelson Mandela (born 1918) was imprisoned in 1962 for his political views, and released only in 1990. In April 1994 he was able to vote for the first time in the country's first free elections. Mandela's party, the African National Congress (ANC), won and he became president.

◀ Black townships in South Africa were disturbed by unrest and violence in the 1980s. Many people were killed and homes set on fire as a tide of protest arose against apartheid.

| 1971 | 1980 | 1985 | 1986 | 1989 | 1993 | 1995 |
|------|------|------|------|------|------|------|
| Swiss women are given the right to vote. | *Solidarity*, an independent trade union, is set up in Poland (banned until 1989). | Marriage between blacks and whites is made legal in South Africa. | Fighting in black townships in South Africa by civil rights protesters. | In Beijing, China, government troops crush a student demonstration for greater democracy. | Nelson Mandela and F W de Klerk win the Nobel peace prize for their work to end apartheid. | Fourth World Conference on Women, held in Beijing, with women present from 185 countries. |

130

# The Vietnam War

VIETNAM, together with Cambodia and Laos, was part of the French colony of Indochina. It was occupied by the Japanese in World War II. During this time the Viet Minh league, led by the Communist Ho Chi Minh, declared Vietnam independent from France.

◀ Ho Chi Minh (1892–1969) led Vietnam's struggle for independence from France. As president of North Vietnam from 1954 he fought for a united Vietnam, achieved after his death.

AFTER the war, France refused to recognize Ho Chi Minh's government and war broke out between the French and the Vietnamese. This war ended in defeat for the French at the battle of Dien Bien Phu in 1954. An international agreement then divided Vietnam into Communist North and non-Communist South.

Almost immediately civil war broke out. From 1959, Communist guerrillas in the South, known as the Viet Cong, were helped by North Vietnam. The USA, anxious to prevent the spread of Communism, sent military aid to the South Vietnamese. The Viet Cong's guerrilla tactics were hard to combat. In an attempt to cut off their supply lines, US planes bombed North Vietnam. Villages in the south and vast areas of forest were sprayed with chemicals to destroy any Viet Cong hiding places. Many civilians were killed.

In 1968, the Viet Cong's Tet offensive in the South convinced most

▶ US soldiers in Vietnam were dropped in by helicopter so that they could make surprise attacks on the Viet Cong guerrilla fighters.

| 1946 | 1954 | 1961 | 1964 | 1965 | 1966 |
|---|---|---|---|---|---|
| Start of the war between Ho Chi Minh's Vietnamese nationalists and French colonial troops. | Vietnamese Communists defeat the French at Dien Bien Phu. The country is divided into North Vietnam and South Vietnam. | South Vietnamese ask for military advice from the USA to combat Communist Viet Cong guerrillas. | War between North Vietnam (backed by the USSR) and South Vietnam (backed by the USA). | USA sends combat troops to South Vietnam. | Australian troops arrive in Vietnam to fight with US troops. The first anti-war demonstrations take place in the USA. |

> Viet Cong and North Vietnamese soldiers used guerrilla warfare. One tactic was to dig a maze of tunnels. Over 16,000 soldiers lived underground, hiding from US planes.

^ Most of the war was fought in the jungles of South Vietnam. The Ho Chi Minh trail, from China through Laos into South Vietnam, was the Viet Cong's supply line from the North.

## ANTI-WAR DEMONSTRATIONS

The Vietnam War was the first to be widely covered on television. People were able to see events as they happened. As growing numbers of US troops were killed or injured, people took to America's streets in protest. By 1967, the protests had spread beyond the USA. The strength of anti-war feeling helped persuade President Richard Nixon to withdraw from the war.

Americans that the war could not be won. In 1969 the USA began to withdraw its troops and a cease-fire was agreed in 1973. Fighting continued until 1975, when North Vietnamese troops took over the South. Vietnam was united.

Most Vietnamese lived by farming, mostly growing rice in the fields around their villages. Many suffered greatly in the war as crops and villages were destroyed.

| 1967 | 1968 | 1969 | 1971 | 1973 | 1975 | 1976 |
|---|---|---|---|---|---|---|
| Peace moves fail. Anti-war demonstrations spread to other countries. | North Vietnamese and Viet Cong launch an attack known as the Tet offensive against the South. Some Americans believe that the war could go on for many years. | The USA withdraws 25,000 of its 540,000 troops. The fighting – and the anti-war protests – continue. | Fighting spreads to Laos. | Cease-fire. US troops withdraw. Vietnamese continue to fight. | Communists take control of South Vietnam. | Vietnam is reunited under a Communist government. |

# China's New Power

132

**W**HEN the Communists, led by Mao Zedong, won power in China, they set out to modernize the country. Their aim was to provide food, schools, hospitals and work for China's millions. These plans were blown off course in the 1960s by Mao's "Cultural Revolution". Later leaders were less radical, but refused to allow the people more freedom or democracy.

◁ The little red book containing the "thoughts of Chairman Mao" was carried by every Red Guard during the turmoil of the Cultural Revolution in China.

THE COMMUNISTS gave women the same rights as men and shared out land among the peasants. They built roads and railways, factories and power stations. In the "Great Leap Forward", every village was meant to be self-sufficient, growing its own food and producing clothes and tools in small factories. But the policies failed, and after bad harvests and mass starvation, Mao retired.

▷ This poster of a triumphant Mao appeared in 1949, when he first came to power. Civil war had left the country in financial disorder. Mao's initial reforms, called the Five Year Plan, helped to improve China's economy.

Mao returned to power in 1966, determined that China should not lose its revolutionary spirit (as he thought had happened in the USSR). He set in progress the Cultural Revolution, with the aim of overthrowing the old China. All his youthful followers carried his little red

**1949**
Mao Zedong's Communist party takes power in China.

**1953**
In the Five Year Plan, peasants are encouraged to set up collective (cooperative) farms.

**1958–1960**
The Great Leap Forward. It is abandoned when its policies result in widespread famine.

**1959**
Mao Zedong retires as Chairman of the Chinese Communist party.

**1966**
Mao sweeps back to power and starts the Cultural Revolution. By 1968 factory productivity is 12 per cent lower than it was in 1966.

**1973**
Rivalry grows between Mao's supporters, known as the "Gang of Four", and Deng Xiaoping over who will succeed Mao.

◀ During the Cultural Revolution, schools and colleges were closed and teachers and students forced to work on the land. Opposition was brutally put down by Red Guards.

▶ Deng Xiaoping (1904–1995) ruled China from 1977 until his death. He reopened contacts with the outside world and encouraged China's economy to grow by setting up privately owned factories.

...ook for inspiration. Traditional customs ...nd thinking were prohibited. Foreigners ...nd old people were insulted. College ...rofessors and teachers were turned out ...f their jobs to work in the fields. ...ospitals and factories, left without ...octors and managers, closed.

When Mao died in 1976, his revolution ended. His successor was Deng Xiaoping, who set up trade links with the outside world and encouraged Chinese business. This policy continued under the next leader, Jiang Zemin. China began to prosper again, but the government was still hesitant to allow political freedom and showed little regard for human rights. Student protests in 1989 were brutally crushed.

◀ Tiananmen Square, Beijing, full of students demonstrating for democracy in May 1989. The Chinese government sent in troops and tanks to clear the protesters and many people were killed.

| ...74 | 1976 | 1977 | 1989 | 1995 |
|---|---|---|---|---|
| ...hina tests ...s first ...clear ...eapons. | Death of Mao. He is briefly succeeded by the Gang of Four, who want to continue the Cultural Revolution. | Deng Xiaoping comes to power. He visits the United States. | Tiananmen Square demonstration by pro-democracy students. | Death of Deng Xiaoping. China's next leader, Jiang Zemin (to 2002), modernizes its economy. |

# Middle East in Crisis

THE MIDDLE EAST has been a world troublespot since 1948, when an uneasy peace followed the Arab-Israeli war. Israel fought three more wars against its Arab neighbours, and the Palestinians remained without a homeland of their own. Terrorism became a terrible weapon in this conflict, which was bound up with two other issues: the world's thirst for oil, much of which comes from Middle East states, and the rise of Islamic fundamentalism.

◀ Ayatollah Khomeini (1900–1989) was a revolutionary religious leader of Iran. He came t power in 1979 after the Sh of Iran was overthrown. Under Khomeini, Iran became a strictly Muslim state.

ISRAEL'S POPULATION increased during the 1950s as Jews emigrated from Europe, Russia and the USA. The Palestinian Arabs, pushed into separate communities within Israel, began a campaign for their own state.

Wars were fought in 1956, 1967 and 1973. The first war began after Egypt took control of the Suez Canal. Britain and France invaded Egypt, but later withdrew. Israel also attacked Egypt. In the Six-Day War in 1967 Israel won control of all Jerusalem, the West Bank of the Jordan river and other territory. It fought off Egyptian and Syrian attacks in the Yom Kippur War of 1973.

▼ Beirut, the capital of Lebanon, was ravaged by fighting that broke out in 1976. Peace returned to the historic city in the mid-1990s.

| 1956 | 1964 | 1967 | 1973 | 1976 | 1979 | 1980–1988 |
|---|---|---|---|---|---|---|
| Egypt takes control of the Suez Canal. | Formation of the Palestinian Liberation Organization (PLO). | Six-Day War, between Israel and Egypt, Jordan and Syria, is won by Israel. | The Yom Kippur War. Israel fights Egypt and Syria. | Fighting breaks out in Lebanon. | Peace treaty between Israel and Egypt. Shah of Iran is overthrown and Islamic republican government set up. | Iran–Iraq War. |

The USA has tried to mediate in the Middle East, though many Arabs see America as Israel's ally. In 1993, President Bill Clinton (centre) welcomed a deal between Israeli Prime Minister Yitzhak Rabin (left) and Yasser Arafat, leader of the Palestinians, to establish Palestinian self-rule. Rabin was assassinated in 1995.

Israel also became involved in the civil war in Lebanon, where many Palestinians lived in refugee camps. By the 1990s, Israel had signed peace agreements with Egypt, Jordan and Syria, and the Palestinians had attained limited self-government. Yet terrorist attacks by extremist groups opposed to new Israeli settlements, and even Israel's very existence, continued.

In 1979 the Shah of Iran was overthrown and an Islamic regime took over. Iran went to war with Iraq in 1980. Neither side won a costly conflict. In 1990 Iraq tried to take over its tiny neighbour Kuwait, but was defeated in the brief Gulf War by a UN force led by the USA. Iraq's ruler Saddam Hussein was finally deposed in 2003, when US-led forces invaded Iraq.

Saddam Hussein (born 1938) ruled oil-rich Iraq from 1979 to 2003. A brutal dictator, he took his people into three wars: against Iran in 1980-1988, and against US-led forces in 1991 and 2003.

| 1982 | 1987 | 1990–1991 | 1993 | 1994 | 1995 | 2003 |
|---|---|---|---|---|---|---|
| Israel invades Lebanon. | Fighting between Palestinians and Israeli troops in the West Bank and Gaza Strip. | In the Gulf War, Iraq invades Kuwait, but is repulsed by UN troops. | Israeli and Palestinian leaders hold talks in the USA. | Israel and Jordan sign a peace agreement. | Israel signs an agreement to extend self-rule to the Palestinians. | Short war in Iraq removes Saddam Hussein. Middle East peace hopes flicker. |

# The Cold War Ends

THE COLD WAR, a time of suspicion, spies and super-missiles, began to look less dangerous in the 1970s. The United States and the Soviet Union found they could agree on some things, such as cutting their arms bills, and signed agreements. The pressure on the Soviet leader was intense; his Communist empire was cracking apart.

The Berlin Wall was demolished in 1989 after the collapse of Communism in East Germany. It had divided the city since 1961. People took pieces as souvenirs.

IN 1972 the USA and USSR signed the first SALT (missile disarmament) agreement. By 1980 the Russians had become involved in a long and costly war in Afghanistan, and their economy was in a bad way. In 1985, a new leader, Mikhail Gorbachev, set about introducing reforms. He also sought friendship with the West. The US president was Ronald Reagan, elected in 1980 on an anti-Communist stand. He was ready to spend billions of dollars on a defensive missile shield in space. But in 1987 Reagan and his

Many symbols of Communism were destroyed after the Soviet Union broke up. Statues of past leaders such as Lenin were pulled down and used as scrap metal. The Communists had dealt similarly with symbols of tsarist rule in 1917.

McDonald's first restaurant in Moscow. Gorbachev began opening up Russia to Western enterprise. Long queues for new Western fast-food soon built up.

**1967**
The USA, Britain and the Soviet Union sign a treaty banning the use of nuclear weapons in outer space.

**1969**
US President Lyndon B Johnson starts the Strategic Arms Limitation Talks.

**1972**
The first SALT agreement is signed by US President Richard Nixon and Leonid Brezhnev of the Soviet Union.

**1979**
Second SALT agreement is signed by US President Carter and Brezhnev. Soviet troops invade Afghanistan. Margaret Thatcher becomes British prime minister.

## EUROPEAN UNION

The European Union (formerly the European Economic Community) was founded in 1957, when it had six members: France, West Germany, Italy, Belgium, the Netherlands and Luxembourg. One of its main aims was to encourage free trade between member countries. By 2002 it had 15 members, most of whom were using the same money (euros). New members eager to join in 2004 included former Communist countries such as Poland and Hungary.

Czech crowds demonstrate in Prague in 1989. Throughout that year, people across Eastern Europe began to demand democracy and an end to repression.

...ritish ally, Margaret Thatcher, signed an ...mportant agreement with the USSR to ...an medium-range nuclear missiles.

Gorbachev's reforms in the Soviet ...nion led to demands for free elections ... Eastern Europe. By the end of 1989, ...ommunism had collapsed in Poland,

Hungary, East Germany, Czechoslovakia and Romania. In 1990, East and West Germany were reunited and free elections were held in Bulgaria. In August 1991 an attempted coup in the Soviet Union led to the downfall of Gorbachev's government. Boris Yeltsin took over until 1999, when he was succeeded by Vladimir Putin. The Soviet Union broke up, and with its collapse, the Cold War was over. There was just one superpower in the world, the United States of America.

Long-time Communist Mikhail Gorbachev (on the left) and Ronald Reagan (on the right) got on well despite Reagan's hatred of Communism. For the first time in 40 years, there were real smiles between US and Soviet leaders.

| ...81 | 1985 | 1989 | 1990 | 1991 |
|---|---|---|---|---|
| ...onald Reagan ...ecomes US ...resident. He ...creases military ...ending. | Mikhail Gorbachev comes to power in the Soviet Union and starts to make reforms. | Free elections are held in Poland. Communism collapses in Hungary, East Germany, Czechoslovakia and Romania. The Berlin Wall is demolished. | East and West Germany are reunited. Free elections are held in Bulgaria. | A multiparty government is set up in Albania. The Soviet Union is abolished and replaced by 15 independent nations. |

# 21st Century World

▶ Using the Internet, people can communicate and exchange information around the globe, through a network of computers, telephone lines and satellites.

WHEN THE 21st century began, people looked forward to a new millennium (the next 1,000 years). No one could say what kind of new world would take shape. Would computers take over more jobs from people? Scientists have made amazing advances in understanding how the human body works by identifying genes. Could science create new plants or even animals? The events of September 11, 2001, made the world seem more dangerous. Yet there was also hope, for a peaceful, fairer world for all.

THE 20TH CENTURY saw two terrible world wars and many civil wars. It closed with NATO bombing Yugoslavia. Later the Yugoslav leader Slobodan Milosevic was put on trial for war crimes – the first time that a head of state had been brought to court in this way. Regional conflicts were caused by ethnic or religious quarrels, or by the desire of one group to break away from a country.

The danger hardest to fight came from terrorists. The world's strongest nation, the United States, was attacked in 2001 by terrorists belonging to the Al-Qaeda organization, who struck at the heart of New York City and Washington, DC. American forces, with support from other nations, attacked Afghanistan, thought to be the hiding place of the terrorist leader Osama Bin Laden.

◀ In modern wars, air power and hi-tech weapons may be used alongside the guns and rocket launchers of local fighters, as in Afghanistan in 2001.

| 1986 | 1998 | 1999 | 1999 | 2000 | 2000 | 2000 |
|------|------|------|------|------|------|------|
| First US patent on a genetically engineered plant – a variety of maize. | A cease-fire is agreed in Northern Ireland. A new power-sharing assembly is set up. | Vladimir Putin becomes leader of Russia. | By this year the Commonwealth of Nations has 54 members – 33 of them are republics. | Hispanic Americans are the largest minority group in the USA. | Data from the US Global Surveyor suggests that Mars may have water – vital for any future manned exploration. | The US presidential election ends in a legal row over ballots. George W Bush wins. |

The United Nations relies on debate and agreement before taking action against a nation. It sent weapons inspectors into Iraq to seek out "weapons of mass destruction" (nuclear, chemical and germ weapons). UN members disagreed about whether war against Iraq, or any "rogue state", was justified.

The Middle East continues to be a troublespot in the 21st century. Political disagreements can sometimes be settled in one meeting between leaders with vision and a realization that compromise is usually needed. Other problems take effort from many people. Hopes for the

**SECRETS OF THE GENE**
The study of the DNA molecule (right) opened the door to genetic engineering — changing living things by altering their genetic makeup.

21st century would be to reduce the gap between the richest nations and the poorest, to fight ignorance and disease, to combat the menace of illegal drugs, and to protect the Earth's natural resources.

The world is rich enough to support even today's population of over 6 billion. But never before in human history has it seemed so small and under such pressure. Humans may visit Mars in the next 100 years, but there is no nearby planet like Earth to move to. *Homo sapiens* has to live in, and conserve, the world our prehistoric ancestors first explored.

We must keep a balance between development (which too often means recklessly cutting down rainforests) and conservation, preserving the Earth's natural riches for all to share.

New York City's World Trade Center towers fell to horrifying terrorist attacks in 2001.

| 2000 | 2001, 11 September | 2001 | 2002 | 2002 | 2002 | 2002 |
|---|---|---|---|---|---|---|
| Scientists have almost completed a map of the human genome. | Terrorists fly airliners into the World Trade Center and Pentagon in the USA. Nearly 3,000 people are killed in the attack. | US-led forces invade Afghanistan and remove the Taliban government. | The European Union starts to use its new currency, the euro, in coins and notes, though Britain is not yet using the euro. | The African Union sets up its own parliament. | Queen Elizabeth II celebrates 50 years as Britain's queen. The Queen Mother dies aged 101. | Former Communist Warsaw Pact members are allowed to join NATO. |

# Acknowledgements

*The publishers wish to thank the following for supplying photographs for this book:*

Page 7 (TL) Bridgeman Art Library; 17 (CR) ( AFF/AFS Amsterdam, the Netherlands, (BR) Mary Evans Picture Library; 11 (BR) The Stock Market; 15 (BL) The Stock Market; 16 (CL) Dover Publication; 19 (CL) AKG London; 20 (BL) AKG London; 27 (TL) Dover Publications; 28-29 (CT) AKG London; 29 (C) MacQuitty International Collection; 30 (BL) ET Archive 31 (BR) Skyscan Photo Library; 32 (BL) AKG London; 34-35 (CB) Dover Publications; 36 (BL) Robert Harding Picture Library; 40 (TR) ET Archive; 43 (B) ETArchive; 44-45 (C) Rex Features; 47 (CR) AKG London; 48-49 (C) ET Archive; 49 (BR) AKG London; 55 (CT) AKG London; 62-63 (C) Mary Evans Picture Libary; 63 (CB) ET Archive; 67 (BL) AKG London; 70-71 (CB) AKG London; 71 (CB) AKG London; 73 (CR) Robert Harding Picture Library; 74 (CL) AKG London; 74-75 (BC) ET Archive; 78 (BL) AKG London; 79 (TR) AKG London; 86 (C) ET Archive; 87 (BR) ET Archive; 90-91 (CB) AKG London; 91 (CR) AKG London; 96-97 (C) ET Archive; 98 (B) AKG London; 99 (B) AKG London; 102 (TR) ILN; 103 (C) ILN; 105 (C) ILN; 105 (C) ILN; 106 (TL) ILN; 108 (BL) ILN; 109 (TR) ILN; 112-113 (C) ILN; 113 (CL) ILN; 112-113 (B) ILN; 113 (C) ILN; 114-115 (C) ILN; 115 (CR) ILN; 116-117 (C) Corbis; 119 (C) ILN; 120 (BL) ET Archive, (TR) ILN; 123 (TC), (CR) ILN; 124 (TR) ILN; 126-127 (C) Rex Features; 127 (BC) ILN, (BR) Rex Features; 129 (CR) Rex Features, (CL) Panos Pictures; 131 (CL), (CR) Rex Features; 132 (BL) ET Archive; 132-133 (BC) Panos Pictures; 134-135 (CB) Panos Pictures; 135 (TL) Rex Features; 137 (C), (BR) Rex Features, (BL) Panos Pictures.

All other photographs from Miles Kelly Archives.